Follow Christ

Developing the Lifestyle
of an Intentional Disciple

Follow Christ

Developing the Lifestyle of an Intentional Disciple

Dave Nodar, Father Erik Arnold, Ally Ascosi

Our Sunday Visitor

www.osv.com
Our Sunday Visitor Publishing Division
Our Sunday Visitor, Inc.
Huntington, Indiana 46750

Nihil Obstat:
Msgr. Michael Heintz, Ph.D.
Censor Librorum

Imprimatur:
✠ Kevin C. Rhoades
Bishop of Fort Wayne-South Bend
October 2, 2015

The *Nihil Obstat* and *Imprimatur* are declarations that a work is free from doctrinal or moral error. It is not implied that those who have granted the *Nihil Obstat* and *Imprimatur* agree with the contents, opinions, or statements expressed.

Our Sunday Visitor Publishing Division, Our Sunday Visitor, Inc., 200 Noll Plaza, Huntington, IN 46750; 1-800-348-2440.

ISBN: 978-1-61278-939-2 (Inventory No. T1712)
eISBN: 978-1-61278-942-2
LCCN: 2016935170

Cover design: Amanda Falk
Cover art: Shutterstock

PRINTED IN THE UNITED STATES OF AMERICA

CONTENTS

Introduction

"Follow me."
— Jesus of Nazareth

There's a great scene in the television miniseries *Jesus of Nazareth* where Peter is beginning to realize the full extent of what Jesus requires of every disciple. You see Peter struggling with the reality that Christ is calling him to choose between living for his desires or following Jesus to learn an entirely new way of living that would impact everything—his entire life, all his plans, his lifestyle, occupation, and family.

As we read the Gospels, we see that Peter's life as a disciple was an ongoing process of conversion. He matured in a relationship with Jesus, which was only possible as a result of the Lord's initiative. Jesus chose Peter, drew him into relationship with Himself, and trained him to do the will of a loving Father by proclaiming the kingdom of God in word and power. Ultimately, the Lord Jesus empowered Peter in the Holy Spirit to live this completely new lifestyle and continue His mission.

The call to follow Jesus was not a "once and done" event for Peter, and it won't be for us. Following Christ means growing in relationship with Jesus and His community of disciples. It is critically important in reading the New Testament to see that following Christ is based on God's initiative—His love for us, the forgiveness of sins, and the gift of the Holy Spirit. He sanctifies and empowers us to move outward to share the good news. The Christian life is based on the grace of God that empowers us ***AND* on our response and effort to mature in doing His will.**

Let me illustrate this important truth of God's initiative and the necessity of our effort. A child is born without having anything do with it. She is conceived by her parent's love. She begins life in the nurture of her mother's womb, but when the child is born she has to breathe and draw milk from her mother in order to grow. Similarly, God initiates our calling out of His love. He gives us the grace we need to continue being transformed. However, we must make efforts in concert with his grace to mature in our life in Christ or that life will be stunted, immature, or even die.

If you choose to excel in a sport, in playing a musical instrument, or in a profession, you have to find a competent teacher who can train you in the proper techniques. You must then establish the discipline of regular practice to become proficient in applying these techniques.

According to Thomas M. Sterner, author of *The Practicing Mind*:

> Everything in life worth achieving requires practice. In fact, life itself is nothing more than one long practice session, an endless effort of refining our motions. When the proper mechanics of practicing are understood, the task of learning something new becomes a stress-free experience of joy and calmness, a process which settles all areas in your life and promotes proper perspective on all of life's difficulties.

Now think about this: You and I have the chance to learn from the most intelligent, wise, loving, perfect Teacher who ever lived. And we have the chance to become His student, His disciple! We can be conformed to Jesus in every way: how we relate to God the Father, how we view the world, how we think, how we conduct ourselves, how we relate to others, and how we use our time, gifting, and resources. By His grace and our effort, we can learn to live a joyful life, surrendering more and more over the years to the Lordship of Jesus.

A disciple of Jesus is an ardent follower who not only professes certain truths, attends church, and serves at certain functions, but who also genuinely applies the teaching of Jesus to every aspect of life. He is confidently aware that God's grace is transforming him. Disciples make Jesus and His Church their primary teachers. We learn from them how to love God above all things and how to love others as Jesus loves them. Essentially we learn to live in harmony with the Father's will, just like our elder brother, Jesus (Mt 7:21, 24; Jn 5:19–20). That is what holiness is all about!

Our growth as disciples of Jesus occurs primarily by staying close to Him, by abiding in Him (Jn 15:5). The Lord has given us certain disciplines that help support the work of His grace as we mature as His followers.

In this book, which is based on the ChristLife "Following Christ" DVD series,* Fr. Erik Arnold, Ally Ascosi, and I will look at some of these basic disciplines—disciplines that have characterized the lives of the saints throughout the ages. We devote chapters to essentials such as spending time in personal prayer each day, listening to God in Scripture, the sacraments, forgiving one another, resisting the devil, and more.

If you make these practices a regular part of your life, they will help you to grow in friendship with the Lord. These time-tested disciplines will advance your maturity in relationship with the Lord, His Church, and others.

Growing as a disciple is best done with others who choose to follow Christ and are members of the Church. That's the way the Lord intended it for us as His family. I've had the great privilege and benefit of having relationships with godly people who loved Jesus and helped disciple me in the Christian life. I pray that will also be true for you!

Nearly fifty years ago I had a radical conversion in which the Lord Jesus laid hold of my life in great love, forgiveness, and power.**

Some months later, during a time of personal prayer, I had an experience of the Lord saying internally, "Come follow me." I accepted His call and decided by the help of His grace to become His disciple. For all these years now, I have practiced what we will be teaching in this book. It has helped me to follow Him. He will help you also! If you will commit your life to Jesus as Lord and tell Him you want to make every effort to live as His disciple, He will answer that prayer.

So how do you begin, or renew, your commitment to follow Christ?

First, stop and pray. Honestly talk to Jesus about His call to you to be His disciple. Tell Him of your need for His Holy Spirit to empower you. Let Him know you are going to make every effort to be changed into His likeness (see 2 Cor 3:18; Rom 8:29).

Second, take time after reading each chapter to prayerfully decide how to apply what is taught there. Write down how you intend to apply the teaching as a normal part of your daily life. Then do it. If it is an area such as establishing a daily personal prayer life, and you mess up, just begin again. Get up and go on! Don't stop. Keep reviewing your decisions and how you are doing. Let each particular area become habitual. Establish the area as a routine part of your discipleship lifestyle.

Third, find some other Christians who want to grow as disciples of Jesus and consider applying the teaching of this book together. Gathering together with others is an important means of maturing as a disciple.

Fourth, take time to praise God for the wonders of His grace that are at work in you, helping you to follow Jesus our Lord and make Him known!

We will be praying for you!

Dave Nodar

---

* *Follow Christ* is based on "Following Christ," a video-based course developed and distributed by ChristLife, a ministry in the Archdiocese of Baltimore. For more information about ChristLife and "Following Christ," please turn to the back pages of the book or see our website, www.christlife.org/follow.

** Dave's story of conversion can be found in the book *Discover Christ*, which is available along with other resources at www.christlife.org.

Chapter 1

Daily Personal Prayer

Dave Nodar

Life is full of responsibilities, surprises, and countless opportunities. What are the most important things? What should compel our attention and what shouldn't? What's vital and what's peripheral? Who wouldn't want to know God's answers to these questions?

It just so happens Jesus gave us a pretty clear answer. In Matthew 22:37–40, Jesus gave us the great commandment:

> "You shall love the Lord your God with all your heart, and with all your soul, and with all your mind. This is the great and first commandment. And a second is like it, You shall love your neighbor as yourself. On these two commandments depend all the law and the prophets."

Jesus focused on what is most important: loving God and loving our neighbor. We love because God first loved us. As we experience His love we return that love. Then God impels us to love others, as He loves us. Our love extends outward, through the Great Commission given to us by Jesus to "make disciples of all nations, baptizing them in the name of the Father and of the Son and of the Holy Spirit, teaching them to observe all that I have commanded you." The Great Commission is the purpose of the law, and it's as true for us now as it was for the people who first heard Jesus say it.

Here's a suggestion. When life gets busy, and you feel pushed by too many demands and too much responsibility, remind yourself of the greatest commandment: love God and love others. We are called to love God above all things and love others like Jesus loves them. We do this by growing in relationship with God, and prayer is a vital way to grow in knowing Him.

PRAY AS JESUS PRAYED

"What would Jesus do?" goes the popular saying. The Gospels give us a picture of Jesus as a man in constant motion, moving from place to place, healing the sick, casting out demons, teaching the people, and sparring with His enemies. But it's also clear from the Gospels that Jesus prayed constantly.

Before He chose His disciples, "he continued in prayer to God" (Lk 6:12) all night. After feeding the five thousand with a few loaves and fish, "he went up into the hills by himself to pray" (Mt 14:23). The whole seventeenth chapter of John's Gospel is a long prayer in which Jesus speaks to His Father intimately. In the Garden of Gethsemane He opens His anguished heart to the Father. We read that "being in an agony he prayed more earnestly" (Lk 22:44). At the very beginning of the Gospel of Mark we read, "In the morning, a great while before day, he rose and went out to a lonely place, and there he prayed" (Mk 1:35).

Prayer was a normal ongoing part of Jesus' daily life. Jesus' relationship with the Father was the most important thing in His life. Everything depended on it. To keep it strong, He spent much time alone with His Father in prayer. The *Catechism of the Catholic Church* says, "His words and works are the visible manifestation of his prayer in secret" (CCC 2602).

This intimate relationship Jesus shared with His Father is what Jesus wants for each of us. The disciples saw Jesus praying all the time, and He made it clear that He expected His disciples to pray. No wonder the disciples came to Him and asked, "Teach us to pray." In Matthew 6, prayer is one of the practices He expects will be part of every disciple's life. It is not optional. He doesn't say, "*If* you pray," or "You might pray this way if you have time for it." He says, "*When* you pray," do it like this.

> "You must not be like the hypocrites; for they love to stand and pray in the synagogues and at the street corners, that they may be seen by men. Truly, I say to you, they have their reward. But when you pray, go into your room and shut the door and pray to your Father who is in secret; and your Father who sees in secret will reward you.
>
> "And in praying do not heap up empty phrases as the Gentiles do; for they think that they will be heard for their many words. Do not be like them, for your Father knows what you need before you ask him." (Mt 6:5–8)

"Do what I do," Jesus says. *Shut the door and pray to your Father who is in secret.* This is what Jesus did all the time: private personal prayer, protected time shielded from the gaze of others. *Do not heap up empty phrases as the Gentiles do.* This is how Jesus prayed: intimate conversation with His Father where He opened the deepest recesses of His heart.

Jesus is more interested in the condition of our hearts than in outward signs of piety. Our motivation for praying should be the love of God; it should not be to impress other people (or ourselves). Prayer is the way we grow closer to God and hear His voice. Jesus is not saying that public communal prayer is unnecessary. He often prayed this way. He went to the synagogue "as was his custom" (Lk 4:16). He went to Jerusalem for the high feasts. Public prayer was a normal part of His life, and He expects it to be part of ours as well. But private personal prayer is essential too. It's the lifeblood of our spiritual lives, as it was for Jesus.

There are many forms of prayer that the Church makes available to us. There are rosaries, novenas, inspiration from the saints, the book of Psalms, Liturgy of the Hours, prayer groups, and so on. We also have the source and summit of prayer and communion with God: The Eucharist and the liturgy of the Mass. What I want to share with you in this chapter is the value of daily personal prayer time where you are alone with God.

Jesus wants you to come to Him and learn from Him. He wants to teach you personally. We will learn about God by coming to Him, staying with Him, spending time with Him, listening to Him, and talking to Him. "Learn from me; for I am gentle and lowly in heart" (Mt 11:29).

PRAY IN THE POWER OF THE SPIRIT

The joy of personal prayer opened up for me about forty-five years ago when I surrendered my life to Jesus as Lord. God's love became real for me. I was overwhelmed by His goodness and renewed in the power of His Holy Spirit. I met a God who poured out blessings on me personally, forgave my sins, and empowered me to live a new life. While I had been raised as a Catholic, baptized and confirmed, as a teenager, I moved far away from living as a Christian. When I committed my life to the Lord Jesus, I experienced a baptism of the Holy Spirit that released the power of those sacraments to live a new life.

Shortly after this conversion experience, I went to a workshop on union with God in daily personal prayer. It changed my life.

One of the most important insights I had is that God wants a personal relationship with me. God loves *me*, Dave, a unique human being. He loves you the same way. He wants to know *you*, and He wants you to know *Him*. It's perfectly possible to go through life with a distant, somewhat impersonal relationship with God. Many people do; I did before asking Jesus to be Lord of my life. When the Holy Spirit opened my eyes, I saw that my relationship with God could be something much more intimate than anything I had ever experienced.

VISITING YOUR MOTHER

You develop a personal relationship with someone by spending time with them. If you meet someone you'd like to be friends with, you spend time with that person. If you are falling in love with someone, you go out on dates. You might follow friends on Facebook, but if they are truly good friends you also make sure you do things together like dinner or a ball game. It's the same thing with God. To develop the relationship, you have to spend the time. That's what prayer is—the time you and God spend together.

Spending the time is at least as important in a relationship as any specific thing that happens between two people. In fact, it's probably *more* important. A speaker once said he compares personal prayer to the time we spend with a close family member—your mother, for example. If your mother lives nearby, you might visit her a couple of times a week. Occasionally you will have a deep conversation, but most of the time you will talk about family members, the weather, food, ailments, your work, and the sales at the mall. You might not be very interested in some of this chitchat; you might steal a furtive glance at your watch and wonder how soon you can leave. But something important is growing under the surface. Your bond with your mother is growing stronger and deeper simply by being with her. Intimacy doesn't come through the chitchat; it's coming through the time you spend together.

So the first step in personal prayer is *taking the time*. Go to prayer with the idea you will spend at least a certain amount of time with God. Find some time in your daily schedule and devote it to prayer. Commit yourself to it. If you're just getting started with personal prayer, try committing yourself to fifteen minutes. This time can gradually increase to perhaps thirty to sixty minutes a day. The important thing is to actually spend this time with God even though nothing much seems to be going on.

Give Him the priority time, the time He deserves as God. This time can be in the morning before you are caught up in the busyness of the day. That's the time I like to pray. Other people like to pray at the end of the day before bedtime. Some people pray during the day. The particular time you pray doesn't matter very much; think about what works with your schedule. What matters is making the time, and sticking to it.

The second step is *finding the right place to pray*. For most of us this will be somewhere in our homes. It might be the corner of a spare bedroom, an old couch in the family room downstairs, or a nook in your apartment. It could also be in church after morning Mass. Wherever you choose should be a quiet place, as free from clutter and visual distractions as possible. It's a good idea to stick to the same prayer place every day if you can. Over time it will become your sacred space and when you go there, you're ready to pray.

The next step is identifying *what you should bring to prayer*. This varies considerably from person to person. I'll share what I do. Keep in mind this is only an example of what one man does. I bring a Bible, my journal, a devotional, my planner, a pad, and a pen. I keep the pad around to jot down any distractions—the thoughts that interrupt my focus on God. I've found that I can get rid of distractions more easily if I write them down and tell myself that I'll think about them later. I usually read the daily Scriptures from a devotional, typically *The Word Among Us* magazine, and meditate on their wonderful reflections. I read and underline important Scriptures in my Bible. I use my journal to write any insights— things that the Lord is saying to me.

I always write down what the Lord has spoken to me, any senses or particular things I've offered to Him in prayer. I found this helpful because it's easy to go from a place of faith to a place of unbelief in our lives. A journal allows me to keep a record of God's promises and action in my life. It is a beautiful way to remind myself of His presence and to give thanks to God for the good things He has done.

You will have to adjust your prayer time according to circumstances and seasons in life. Parents of small children will find it difficult to stick to a set prayer time. Illness will keep you in bed. You will travel. There will be times when work and family responsibilities will be so great that you scramble to find time to do everything that needs to be done. By all means make the necessary adjustments to your prayer time. You'll be better able to cope with these pressures if you've already established the habit of regular personal prayer.

Your prayer will change over time. You might want to read more Scripture, spend more time silently listening, less time on something else. Pray about what you should do in prayer. Be led by the Holy Spirit. Be like the old peasant who spent hours before the crucifix in the church pastored by St. John Vianney, the Cure of Ars. One day St. John asked the man what he did in his time of prayer. The peasant said, "I look at Him, and He looks at me."

LORD, TEACH US TO PRAY

Our teacher in prayer is Jesus. When the disciples wanted to know how to pray, they went to the Lord and asked Him. He said:

Pray then like this:

Our Father who art in heaven,
Hallowed be thy name.
Thy kingdom come.
Thy will be done,
On earth as it is in heaven.

Give us this day our daily bread;
And forgive us our trespasses,
As we forgive those who trespass against us;
And lead us not into temptation,
But deliver us from evil.

(Mt 6:9–13)

The Our Father is Jesus' most explicit teaching about prayer. What follows is a part-by-part analysis of what Jesus teaches us in the Our Father (much of this is inspired by Fr. Michael Scanlan's excellent book *Appointment with God*.)

Our Father who art in heaven,
Hallowed be thy name.

The Our Father begins with praise. This is the natural starting point for prayer—praising God for who He is, thanking Him for the many blessings He has showered on us. Jesus praised His Father: "Father, I thank you that you have heard me" (Jn 11:41). "I thank you, Father, Lord of heaven and earth" (Lk 10:21). In the Liturgy of the Hours, the Church praises God throughout the day, every day, everywhere in the world. I like to praise God by praying the Psalms, such as Psalm 105:

O give thanks to the LORD, call on his name,
    make known his deeds among the peoples!
Sing to him, sing praises to him,
    tell of all his wonderful works!
Glory in his holy name;
    let the hearts of those who seek the LORD
        rejoice!
Seek the LORD and his strength,
    seek his presence continually.

(Ps 105:1–4)

Beginning our prayer with praise helps us get in the proper posture before God. He is God and we are His creatures, He is our Father and we are His children. He is our Lord and Savior and we are His disciples!

Thy kingdom come.
Thy will be done,
> *On earth as it is in heaven.*

Next we listen to the Lord and hear what He has to say to us. Scripture is an essential help to hearing God in prayer. Take one of the readings from the Mass of the day, for example, and read it slowly and prayerfully. Ask the Lord to speak to you through it. As I mentioned before, write down any promises from the Lord, words of encouragement, direction, or key Scripture passages.

Sometimes it's hard to tell God, "Thy will be done." It can be a struggle to align your will and God's will. This struggle, the place where our will crosses with the Father's will, is where the cross is applied to our lives. It is what Jesus felt as He was wrestling in Gethsemane before His passion. This is part of a real life of prayer. We come to Him in personal prayer to learn to do His will—Thy will be done.

Give us this day our daily bread.

Next, we surrender our daily needs to God and intercede on behalf of others. The Lord is concerned about you and the things you're concerned about. Jesus says that we should ask the Lord for what we need. We should pray for our needs, the needs of others, and for those of the world. The Father is a real Father—we are His children, and children can freely ask their fathers for what they want. The Lord wants to know your heart and your desires. Personally, in order to help me remain faithful in intercession, I keep a sticky note in the front of my journal with a list of people and things I'm praying for.

And forgive us our trespasses,
      As we forgive those who trespass against us.

Forgiveness is an essential part of following Christ (more on forgiveness in chapter 4). Prayer is real, not imaginary, and in daily prayer we face up to our failures and sins honestly. The Father wants us to take off our masks and be who we are before Him. He already knows who we are. He wants us to know who we are too—sinners in need of forgiveness, but also His children whom He intends to transform from the inside out. We can come to Him and say, "Father forgive me. I need your help."

And lead us not into temptation,
      But deliver us from evil.

Shortly after my conversion I had the rude awakening to the reality that I could still yield to my temptations and fall into sin. I fell to impure thoughts. I was humbled by my weakness especially in light of my new awareness of God's personal love for me. I confessed my sin, and asked the Lord to give me power to obey Him and, when I did fall to temptations, to give me grace to get up and go on with Him.

In this petition we recognize that our human strength is not enough for the trials and temptations that we will face this side of heaven. *Temptations are sure to come*, Jesus tells us. They are common to humanity, and the Father intends to use them to strengthen us, His children, in living for His will as we patiently surrender to His transforming power at work in us. We can pray: "Lord, lead me not into temptation; give me the power of your Spirit to resist temptations and make me holy."

We also recognize in this petition that ultimately the author of all the evils we are prone to is the devil (more on the devil in chapter 8). With humility, we recognize that our Father has absolute authority and that we His children can approach Him for His protection to overcome the enemy. We can have confidence that the Father hears us when we pray like this because the Lord Jesus prayed for us with these words, "I do not pray that you should take them out of the world, but that you should keep them from the evil one" (Jn 17:15).

As we began our prayer time remembering who God is and who we are, we end our time with humility and praise to God our Father, who is Lord of heaven and earth and empowers us to live fully as His children!

Yours is the kingdom and the power and the glory forever and ever. Amen!

As you end your time of prayer, decide how this time with God will influence the rest of your day. What has the Lord said to you? Where do you need God the most? "Blessed rather are those who hear the word of God and keep it!" (Lk 11:28). We resolve to be doers of the Word and not just hearers. Our union with God through personal prayer transforms our hearts and our minds and should also transform our actions.

One last thought about prayer: Don't lose sight of how wonderful the gift of prayer is! Every day you have the opportunity to fall out of bed, shake off the grogginess of sleep, and spend time with God. You can talk to each other. You can tell Him your troubles. You can receive comfort and counsel from Him. You can grow in wisdom and strength and learn how to walk with Christ. He will transform you as you come to be with Him in an ongoing way! What a great gift He offers us!

PRACTICAL APPLICATION TO BECOME "DOERS OF THE WORD"

Begin planning your personal prayer time—time, location, etc. Write down your intentions and talk to the Lord, asking Him for grace to establish a daily personal prayer time as a normal ongoing part of your life.

Chapter 2

Hearing God in Scripture

Fr. Erik Arnold

When I was a kid, we had a great big leather-bound family Bible on a bookshelf in our living room. It was so big you could hardly miss it—but we seldom took it down and opened it. Our family wasn't that different from many other Catholic families. We were told that the Bible was important, but it really wasn't part of our lives. The Bible was there, but it stayed on the shelf.

This chapter is about taking the Bible off the shelf and making it part of your life. Scripture is the Word of God. It has real power. It can bring us freedom and joy and wisdom. God reveals Himself through the words of Scripture, and by reading the Bible prayerfully we can hear God speak directly to us. It's no wonder reading Scripture is a central part of personal prayer.

GOD'S LOVE LETTER

The Bible is entirely unique. It looks like other books—words printed on paper, bound in leather or paper-covered boards, sold in stores or online. But the Bible is a book apart. The other books in the religion section of the bookstore contain other people's ideas about God. The Bible is *God's own Word spoken about Himself.* The Holy Spirit inspired the human authors of the Bible to write what God wanted to communicate. It's a priceless gift to us, given out of love. This is what the *Catechism* has to say about it:

> In Sacred Scripture, the Church constantly finds her nourishment and her strength, for she welcomes it not as a human word, but as what it really is: the word of God. In the sacred books, the Father who is in heaven comes lovingly to meet his children, and talks with them. (CCC 104)

This is the wonder and beauty of Scripture: it flows from the Father's deep desire to open His heart to us so that we can know Him. Scripture flows from God's love. It's one of the greatest of gifts that the Father showers on us. It's no exaggeration to say that Scripture is God's love letter to us.

Because Scripture is God's Word to us, *it is alive with the power of God.* No human words have the power that Scripture has. Think about a time that words have moved you: maybe it was a novel you read as a child, a letter from someone you love, a play that you saw on stage. These words are *human expressions* of love or grief or joy. But the words of Scripture carry the power of God Himself.

> The word of God is living and active, sharper than any two-edged sword, piercing to the division of soul and spirit, of joints and marrow, and discerning the thoughts and intentions of the heart. (Heb 4:12)

These are not generic words. They are personal—aimed at you, at me, and at every person who reads them. They are truly *personal.* In Scripture you can hear God's Word for *you.* You can read a passage and hear what God wants you to hear at that moment. Your spouse or your best friend can read the same verse and hear what *they* need to hear. That's the power of the Word of God.

When we read Scripture, we take our place in the crowd that Luke describes: "While the people pressed upon him to hear the word of God, [Jesus] was standing by the lake of Gennesaret" (Lk 5:1). The people didn't come to Jesus to hear generic, abstract truths. Each of them came to hear Jesus talk to them personally. They recognized that Jesus had something to say to them. We read Scripture for the same reason: God has something to say to *me*, something that I need to hear right now, something for me personally, in the circumstances I'm in, with the needs that I have, the challenges I face, the opportunities I have. There are things that need to be removed from my life. Other things need to be added. We need strength and encouragement. Our eyes need to be opened to see where God is at work. The Lord will talk to us about these things as we read Scripture.

GOD'S WORD HAS POWER

Let me share with you a couple of examples. One of my favorite stories about the power of God's Word comes from the life of St. Augustine, one of the greatest of the early Fathers of the Church.

You're probably familiar with the basic story of Augustine's life. He was a brilliant young man who restlessly searched for love and truth as he made a name for himself as a teacher and writer in the Roman Empire. His mother, Monica, was a fervent Christian, but he resisted her attempts to bring him to faith in Christ. For years he carried on a personal and intellectual struggle. Finally, Augustine became convinced of the truth of the Gospel. He knew that he should accept baptism and become a Christian, but he hesitated at the brink of conversion, embroiled in a spiritual struggle with the sins he knew he had to leave behind:

I was held back by mere trifles, the most paltry inanities, all my old attachments. They plucked at my garment of flesh and whispered, "Are you going to dismiss us? From this moment we shall never be with you again, for ever and ever. From this moment you will never again be allowed to do this thing or that, for evermore."

They no longer barred my way, blatantly contradictory, but their mutterings seemed to reach me from behind, as though they were stealthily plucking at my back, trying to make me turn my head when I wanted to go forward. Yet, in my state of indecision, they kept me from tearing myself away, from shaking myself free of them and leaping across the barrier to the other side, where you were calling me. Habit was too strong for me when it asked, "Do you think you can live without these things?" (*Confessions* VIII, 11)

In spiritual agony, Augustine cried out to the Lord. How long? How long is it to be? He describes what happened next:

As I was saying this and weeping in the bitter agony of my heart, suddenly I heard a voice from a nearby house chanting as if it might be a boy or a girl ... saying and repeating over and over again, "Pick up and read, pick up and read." At once my countenance changed, and I began to think intently whether there might be some sort of children's game in which such a chant was used. But I could not remember having heard of one.... I interpreted it solely as a divine command to open the book [a copy of the letters of St. Paul] and read the first chapter I might find. (*Confessions* VIII, 12)

His eyes landed on a passage from Romans:

> Let us conduct ourselves becomingly as in the
> day, not in reveling and drunkenness, not in
> debauchery and licentiousness, not in quarreling
> and jealousy. But put on the Lord Jesus Christ,
> and make no provision for the flesh, to gratify its
> desires. (Rom 13:13–14)

The passage told Augustine something that he had known for some time—that he needed to leave the old life behind and accept the new life of Christ in baptism. But now the conviction moved from his head to his heart. In a flash, he received the power he needed to act on what he knew to be true. Augustine was soon baptized and became a Christian. Where did Augustine find the power to overcome the fears and doubts that had plagued him for so long? Not from himself. The power came from the Word of God in Scripture.

Here we discover one of the most important differences between God's Word and mere human words: God's Word contains in itself the power to accomplish the very things it declares. Unlike the latest self-help book, which may have good advice for my life but leaves me to do the work, God's Word is able to make happen exactly what it proclaims. This opens up for us a whole new way of reading Scripture—a way in which we expect God's Word to accomplish in us the very thing we are reading!

GOD'S WORD GIVES DIRECTION

Because Scripture is alive in this way, it can also point us in the right direction. It can help us answer the questions we have. It can tell us things we need to know. This happened to me at a crisis point in my own life.

It happened about half way through my first year in diocesan seminary. At that time, many seminaries had not experienced the spiritual reform that has since taken place. I had entered seminary after a careful discernment process, and I was as sure as I could be that God was calling me to be a diocesan priest. But as the year went on, the various struggles in the seminary left me restless and unsettled. I wasn't sure I was in the right place. I thought I should be a priest, but perhaps I should join a religious order instead of becoming a diocesan priest. The struggle was so intense that I even began visiting different religious orders.

At some point in the midst all of this it dawned on me that I couldn't make the decision on my own. Even though I was tempted to pack up my room and leave, I was drawn instead to make a special novena asking the Lord to guide me in the direction I should go. At the end of the nine days, I had a strong sense that the Lord wanted me to look into Scripture for some wisdom about my problem. I was led to a beautiful passage from Isaiah:

> By waiting and by calm you shall be saved,
> in quiet and in trust shall be your strength.
> But this you did not will.
>
> "No," you said,
> "Upon horses we will flee."
> Very well, you shall flee!
> "Upon swift steeds we will ride."
> Very well, swift shall be your pursuers!
> (Is 30:15–16, NABRE)

These words spoke to me immediately. The Lord was telling me to wait, to trust Him and be calm, not to rush into the wrong decision: "in quiet and in trust shall be your strength." But He also convicted me when, in the same passage, He said: "But this you did not will." He was right. I was ready to leave, to flee, not to wait and be calm. I understood very clearly that the Lord was telling me not to make any decision about my future now, but to wait trustingly.

So I waited. And about two months later, out of the blue, the Director of Vocations for the Archdiocese called to tell me that the Archbishop wanted to send me to a different seminary to complete my formation. I was shocked and surprised, but I saw this clearly as God's hand at work, so I accepted the transfer. The five years of seminary that followed my transfer were among the most blessed of my life and culminated in my ordination as a priest for the Archdiocese of Baltimore, which is exactly where the Lord wanted me.

See what I mean when I say that Scripture is alive with the power of God? God was waiting for me when I opened the Bible to Isaiah, chapter 30. It was His will that I stay on the path I was on and eventually serve as a parish priest. At that time of crisis He was waiting to give me direction about an important decision, but He's *always* waiting for me when I open the Scriptures. He's waiting for you too.

GOD'S WORD SPOKEN AT MASS

There are many ways to make Scripture part of your life. The most important way—one sometimes overlooked—is the proclamation of the Word of God at Mass. Christ comes to us in two ways at Mass: in Scripture (the Liturgy of the Word) and in His Body and Blood (the Liturgy of the Eucharist). The culmination of the Liturgy of the Word at every Mass is the proclamation of the Gospel, the very words and deeds of Christ Himself. This is preceded by a reading from the Old Testament, which tells us of God's promises and preparation of His people for the coming of His Son, and by a responsorial psalm. This is followed by a reading from the letters of St. Paul, the Acts of the Apostles, and other pastoral letters proclaiming the message of Christ to the early Christian community.

As we said earlier, God's Word has unique power to do the very thing it proclaims. This is especially true in the celebration of the Mass. Our bishops put it this way:

> The Word of God proclaimed in the Liturgy possesses a special sacramental power to bring about in us what it proclaims. The Word of God proclaimed at Mass is "efficacious," that is, it not only tells us of God and God's will for us, it also helps us to put that will of God into practice in our own lives.*

Think about that for a moment. At Mass, Scripture does what it's describing. The Old Testament reading is preparing us to receive Christ. The reading from St. Paul, Acts, or another pastoral letter is proclaiming the message to us personally. The Gospel reading is bringing salvation and healing to us as it tells of the words and deeds of Christ.

So, imagine you are at Mass and the Gospel reading is the parable of the prodigal son (Lk 15:11–32). In the very act of hearing that beautiful Gospel, which describes the merciful heart of our heavenly Father, that very mercy is being poured out on you and made real for you. You are not just hearing about God's mercy, you are actually receiving it as it's being proclaimed!

It makes sense then to pay especially close attention to the Scripture readings at Mass, expecting the power of God's Word to be at work. A good practice is to read these passages ahead of time in order to prepare your heart. Good commentaries can also be helpful in preparing our hearts. The monthly magazine *The Word Among Us* provides the daily and Sunday Scripture readings with powerful and practical commentaries. You can also get the day's reading by email every morning from the United States Conference of Catholic Bishops by signing up at www.usccb.org/bible/readings/.

GOD'S WORD IN YOUR LIFE

To make Scripture a part of your daily prayer, it's important to work from a good readable translation of the Bible. There are dozens of English translations and hundreds of editions available, ranging from thick scholarly commentaries to small editions of the Gospels that you can slip into the pocket of your jeans. For personal prayer, the two most common translations for Catholics are the New American Bible (which is the translation used at Mass) and the Catholic edition of the Revised Standard Version. Study and application editions are available for both of these that offer footnotes and sidebars that help explain the text.

If you aren't in the habit of reading Scripture regularly, it might be helpful to start with the daily Mass readings or praying through one of the Gospels. Read for five or ten minutes a day, then more as time permits and the Holy Spirit leads. Focus on Jesus, and as you're reading, ask: What does He do? What does He say? What kind of a man is He? Be alert to what God is saying to you through the words of Scripture. You're not reading the Bible in order to get information into your head. You're reading in order to encounter God personally. What is the living Word of God in Scripture saying to your heart?

A method that helps us read Scripture with our hearts is an ancient practice called *Lectio Divina* (Latin for "Divine Reading"). This is slow, meditative reading of a single passage several times for the purpose of discerning its inner meaning for us personally. The four traditional steps of Lectio are reading, meditation, prayer, and contemplation. The text is first read for meaning. This leads to meditation, where we seek to hear God's voice in the passage. Then comes prayer, our intimate conversation with God. Finally, the text takes us into contemplation. "Words in this kind of prayer are not speeches; they are like kindling that feeds the fire of love" (CCC 2717).

There are many variations to *Lectio Divina*. Often, the four traditional steps blend into one process of ever-deepening understanding and prayer.

Following the example of the saints, one of the most powerful ways to read Scripture is to use our imagination to construct the entire scene, allowing the Holy Spirit to bring it to life in our hearts and minds. As an example, suppose you are reading the account of the healing of the blind man Bartimaeus (Mk 10:46–52). Place yourself in the scene. You are a bystander in the crowd watching these amazing events take place. You're sweating in the hot sun. You smell the dust kicked up in the road. You're jostled by other people in the crowd as everybody strains to see what's going on. You hear Bartimaeus cry out to Jesus, and you hear the people in the crowd trying to shut him up. Then you keenly watch what Jesus does. You notice His tone of voice, His body language, His gestures as He asks the blind man, "What do you want me to do for you?" And you imagine Jesus asking you the same question, "What do you want me to do for you?" In that moment, as you respond, your prayer shifts to a deeply personal place in your own heart as you share with Jesus what you most hope and long for Him to do for you.

Imaginative reading is a powerful way to come to know Jesus. He is not just a historical figure who stirred the crowds and alarmed the authorities two thousand years ago. He is alive now in the Gospels, and He wants to come to save and heal *you*.

---

* "Hearing the Word of God," at www.usccb.org/prayer-and-worship/the-mass/order-of-mass/liturgy-of-the-word/hearing-the-word-of-god.cfm

PRACTICAL APPLICATION TO BECOME "DOERS OF THE WORD"

As you read Scripture prayerfully, you will be meeting the Lord again and again, day after day, month after month. In these daily encounters with the Lord it's important not to lose track of what he is saying to you.

Write down how the Lord is speaking during your personal prayer time and through your reading of Scripture. Our prayer time is meant to have an incredibly practical effect on our lives: to teach and empower us to follow the Lord Jesus.

What a blessing and delight it can be to go through your prayer journal and see how much God has done for you and through you over the years and all of the ways he has come to you and changed you by the power of his Word.

Chapter 3

The Power of the Sacraments

Ally Ascosi

I'm a list person. I simply love making lists. Most people I know keep all their to-do's electronically, whether on their phones or computers, but if you ask me, there is something almost thrilling about a blank legal pad just waiting to be filled by the day's tasks; a pad where you can cross out each item by hand and get that feeling of pure satisfaction. This is a book about putting together all the elements of a healthy Christian life. There is a great list, right there, in the table of contents—prayer, Scripture, sacraments, forgiveness, and all the rest. But there's a danger in doing what we're doing: we can get the idea that following Christ is a matter of making the perfect list and working very hard to check off everything on it. Personal prayer, check. Reading Scripture, check. Service to others, check. Although checking off each item might seem satisfying, if we're not careful, we might think that the most important part of following Jesus is our own effort. That's honestly what I thought. When I became a Catholic, my senior year of high school, I thought it was all about my choosing Him. And the next year, when I went off to college, I made my perfect checklist and included everything I needed to do to keep following Him.

The truth is that everything on that list comes about through God's initiative, not ours. Jesus said, "You did not choose me, but I chose you" (Jn 15:16). God has been inviting you to know Him and love Him from the moment you were born. This very moment, He is reaching out to you—as you are reading these words. He will always reach out to you; His love never ends. When you surrendered your life to God, it was because His grace gave you the power to do so. And now you are able to follow Christ because His grace is alive in you. The *Catechism* says, "Grace is … the *free undeserved help* that God gives to us to respond to his call to become children of God" (CCC 1996, emphasis in original). Our effort isn't enough; He gives us the help we need to respond to His call. My effort wasn't enough either, my perfect list wasn't enough, but thankfully His grace is.

MY SURRENDER TO GOD

I became Catholic during my senior year of high school. I went off to college feeling pretty confident, but then I found that the Christian life felt like a burden compared to the party life I saw all around me. My life soon got out of control, and I blamed everyone but myself—I blamed my father who left when I was young, bad friends and relationships, and even God.

The summer before my junior year, after blacking out at a party, I providentially found some of my old Christian friends, and they took me home. I realized what could have happened to me, and it felt like a second chance. I remember looking at myself in the mirror the next day saying, "Who are you?" and I realized I needed to change my life.

I found the strength to change my life—not through my own willpower, but through surrendering my life to God. I returned to the sacraments and received deep healing from sin, depression, selfishness, and feeling unlovable. God gave me the power to forgive my father and to live my life completely for Him.

Nothing reminds me more clearly of God's initiative to help us live a Christian life than His gift of the sacraments. Thankfully, Jesus didn't just say, "Follow me," and then leave us hanging. But rather Jesus gave us the sacraments to help us to follow after Him. The grace we receive is all about sharing in Jesus' very life, His divine life.

> God, who is rich in mercy, out of the great love with which he loved us, even when we were dead through our trespasses, made us alive together with Christ (by grace you have been saved). (Eph 2:4–5)

OVERVIEW OF THE SACRAMENTS

The sacraments are the primary way that Christ is alive in us. They don't just point us to God's grace, they truly bring about what they signify. God chose to use tangible, everyday things—water, oil, bread, wine—to give His life. Baptism, for example, is not only an exterior cleansing that symbolizes interior cleansing, but it actually produces the cleansing of our souls, our rebirth in Christ.

Jesus gave us seven sacraments. Three—Baptism, Confirmation, and Eucharist—are the foundational sacraments. The Church calls them the sacraments of initiation because these sacraments bring us into the life of Christ and continue to sustain us. The other sacraments are Reconciliation, Matrimony, Holy Orders, and Anointing of the Sick.

While all of the sacraments are equally important, the Eucharist and Reconciliation are the sacraments that we will experience most in our day-to-day lives as Christians. The rest of this chapter will focus upon these two sacraments and their power to transform our lives.

THE EUCHARIST

The Church says that the Eucharist is the "source and summit of the Christian life" (CCC 1324). The Eucharist is like a diamond. It's rather unimpressive on its own, but it's spectacular when placed in a beautiful setting. It becomes the focal point, attracts attention, and brings light to everything around it. The Eucharist was given to us not to be isolated, but to be placed in the setting of the rest of the Christian life— prayer, Scripture reading, community, and service.

When I first came in contact with the Catholic Church, I was immediately drawn to the Eucharist. I grew up Protestant but started going to Mass with friends while I was in high school. Although I grew up thinking of Communion as a symbolic ritual, the way that the Lord's Supper was made present at a Catholic Mass tugged at my heart powerfully. To me it was stunning to realize that Catholics believed the bread and wine of the Eucharist was Jesus Himself, really present!

If we look to Scripture, Jesus clearly taught us about the Eucharist. In fact, He couldn't have been any clearer: "Truly, truly, I say to you, unless you eat the flesh of the Son of man and drink his blood, you have no life in you;… my flesh is food indeed, and my blood is drink indeed" (Jn 6:53, 55). These words outraged Jesus' enemies, who thought them blasphemous. Even Jesus' friends were puzzled and confused, and many of them left His company because of this radical teaching; what did it mean to eat His flesh and drink His blood? Surely Jesus would have cleared everything up if it was simply a symbol.

In his First Letter to the Corinthians, St. Paul tells the new Christians what happened at the Last Supper:

> For I received from the Lord what I also delivered to you, that the Lord Jesus on the night when he was betrayed took a loaf of bread, and when he had given thanks, he broke it, and said, "This is my

body which is for you. Do this in remembrance of me." In the same way also the chalice, after supper, saying, "This chalice is the new covenant in my blood. Do this, as often as you drink it, in remembrance of me." (1 Cor 11:23–25)

It wasn't just a symbol. Remember, the sacraments produce what they signify; therefore, the bread and wine of the Eucharist don't just point to spiritual nourishment, but they actually nourish us. As Jesus said, He is our heavenly food: "the bread which comes down from heaven, that a man may eat of it and not die" (Jn 6:50). Christians have recognized this from the very beginning. The second chapter of the Acts of the Apostles describes the origins of the Church: The Holy Spirit came at Pentecost, the apostles preached the Gospel, and those who believed were baptized. These new Christians "held steadfastly to the apostles' teaching and fellowship, to the breaking of bread and to the prayers" (Acts 2:42). The breaking of the bread was the Eucharist. It was at the center of the life of the early Church and has remained at the center ever since.

Think of a great festive meal with your closest friends and loved ones. I hope it's more than just a quick fast-food drive-thru in which you get your food and get out. I will never forget the first time I spent Christmas Eve dinner with my husband Peter and his large Italian family. It's called the Feast of the Seven Fishes, and what a joyous feast it was! We ate platter after platter of seafood and pasta, and of course wine. We hardly had room for dessert. But like any great feast, it was about more than the food. There were memories shared, carols sung around my father-in-law playing the accordion, and lots of laughter. The intensity of the joy and intimacy and sharing wouldn't have been possible without the food. It's the same with the Eucharist. The Eucharist is intended to nourish as individuals but also to bring us closer together as brothers and sisters in Christ.

The word Eucharist comes from the Greek word *eucharistia*, which means thanksgiving. It can often be overlooked, but the prayers in the Liturgy of the Eucharist, the second part of the Mass, are mostly prayers of thanksgiving and gratitude. We give thanks for Christ's sacrifice of Himself, that great act of love that brought about our salvation. There's a moment when the priest holds up the host and says, "Behold the Lamb of God." It's a moment of great solemnity when we can receive life from the Lord, a time when we bow before Him in gratitude and let His love and mercy penetrate our hearts. A priest friend of mine says, "That moment is just too short." That's why we have Eucharistic Adoration, where we can prolong that moment and spend more time worshipping and thanking Jesus for the awesome gift of Himself.

The Eucharist is often referred to as "Communion" because it is a very important sign of our unity. "Because there is one bread, we who are many are one body, for we all partake of the one bread," St. Paul wrote to the Corinthians (1 Cor 10:17). The Eucharist is the glue that binds us together in the Church. Catholics are celebrating the same Eucharist all over the world. They are celebrating the same Eucharist in slums and suburbs, in deserts and airports, in nursing homes and universities. This unity is such a treasure that I have found in the Catholic Church, especially in light of a world torn apart by divisions, including the divisions among Christians. And yet it is the Father's heart that "they may all be one" (Jn 17:21), and so I make a point to pray like Jesus did for the unity of all Christians.

Jesus is fully present in the Eucharist—Body, Blood, Soul, and Divinity. And He desires to be fully present to us, to meet us, to speak to us, to minister to us. Jesus said, "He who eats my flesh and drinks my blood abides in me, and I in him" (Jn 6:56). The Eucharist is how Jesus is with us; He is with us in the closest way. Although, in faith, I know this is always true, occasionally I have moments when I especially feel this intimacy. Once, I went to Mass with the burden of an unresolved decision that was causing me a great deal of anxiety. I wasn't able to focus or even listen to the homily because I was distracted. But after I received the Eucharist, a peace flooded over me. My circumstance didn't change; I still had a decision to make, but the weight was gone. I felt God's peace, as if He said, "Everything's going to be okay, Ally." Sometimes during that quiet time after I receive the Eucharist, a Scripture of encouragement comes to my mind or I get an idea of how to serve someone who needs help. God is giving us His grace, His life, to work in us if we let it.

Have you ever had a profound distraction during Mass? Anxiety or worry? Have you taken that time right after Communion to let Jesus speak to you, minister to you? Or have you let the distraction win? I used to wonder, "What do people pray, just kneeling here?" But then I realized that it's a very important time for God to speak to me. And so, I encourage you, the next time you go to Mass spend some time listening to the Lord in those quiet moments after Communion. He's really present in you. He wants to meet you there, in the silence of your heart.

PENANCE AND RECONCILIATION

Wouldn't it be wonderful if we could live our whole lives in the intimacy with Jesus that we have in the moments after Communion? Yes it would. But we don't do it. We pull away. We fail in our responsibilities, let other people down, cut corners, give into pressure, disguise the truth, lash out at others, and abuse others and ourselves. We fall short constantly, every day, in large things and in small things. This is sin—our failure to be the people God wants us to be. And it breaks our communion with God.

Fortunately, God wants us back. He is ready to forgive. In *The Joy of the Gospel*, Pope Francis profoundly reminds us, "God never tires of forgiving us; we are the ones who tire of seeking his mercy" (3). This is what happens in the Sacrament of Reconciliation. We bring our burden of sin to God. If we repent of our sin and ask forgiveness, God will lift our burden from us—and then He will forget about it. Why does He do this? The *Catechism* explains: "The whole power of the sacrament of Penance consists in restoring us to God's grace and joining us with him in intimate friendship" (CCC 1468). Pretty wonderful, huh?

It is wonderful, yet we often resist it. To tell you the truth, for me, Reconciliation was the biggest barrier to becoming Catholic. I didn't want to tell my sins to a priest. I thought that it was embarrassing and shameful. Let's take a look the parable of the Prodigal Son, a story Jesus told about reconciliation. This son cut ties with his father by taking his inheritance and blowing it. Let's just say it wasn't long before he was down in the dirt. But it wasn't until he was eating from a pig's trough that he thought of his father and said, "I'm going to go home; being a servant for Him is better than this!" The whole way home, he's running all the sins through his head—all the things he did wrong and what he's going to say. Sound familiar? When he gets to the gate, his father is already there to meet him. He's there to welcome him, embrace him, love him. That's how we need to think of this sacrament. Yes, we are bringing all our sins, our failures, everything we are ashamed of. But the Lord is already there. He is at the gate, waiting to welcome us. He loves us that much!

THE THREE PARTS OF RECONCILIATION

Confession is the term commonly used for the sacrament, but the confession of our sins to a priest is only one part of the process. The others are *contrition* and *penance*.

The first part is *contrition*, or *repentance*. Repentance means changing direction. It's the willingness to be honest about what we have done. In a way, this is the most important part of the sacrament. God longs to receive us back. But that isn't the issue. The issue is whether we are honest enough to turn to Him to forgive us. We can't fix ourselves before we go to Him. We need to run to Him in our mess and let Him to do the fixing.

The next part is *confession*. For most people this is the hardest part. It's hard to tell someone else what you've done wrong. But taking the time to self-reflect and externalize what is inside of us allows for growth. Before I go to the sacrament, I always spend several minutes in prayer and write down all that I desire to confess. This allows me to give a thorough, heartfelt confession. Afterward, it feels so good to tear up that paper or better yet throw it in a roaring fire.

Many people recognize the importance of confessing their sins, but still ask the question: why do we have to go to a priest? While God is the only one who can forgive sins, He chooses to forgive us using another tangible sign: a person! A person who stands in His place. A person who isn't merely a person, just like the water of baptism isn't merely water, or the bread and wine of the Eucharist aren't merely bread and wine. No, this person is Jesus Himself, forgiving you through His minister, a priest. Jesus gave this authority to His apostles before He ascended (Jn 20:21). And God knows we need this. We need to hear—from Him—the words of absolution. "May God give you pardon and peace," and "I absolve you from your sins." And finally, this act of confession reconciles us also to the Church community.

The final part of the sacrament is *penance*. He doesn't want us to keep living in our sin. In preparing the way for the coming of Christ, John the Baptist exhorts the crowds, "Bear fruits that befit repentance" (Lk 3:8). In other words, don't just say, "I'm sorry, Lord" and go back to the same way you were living. Rather, repentance should lead to a change of life. After we confess our sins, the priest will recommend a penance—for example, praying certain prayers or performing an act of charity. Penance restores us to "full spiritual health" (CCC 1459). It is *not* a way to earn God's forgiveness, but should be joyfully accepted as evidence of a true interior change of heart.

One powerful encounter I had with Jesus through the sacrament of Reconciliation occurred when I was in college. I had been on a path away from God and the Church and was numbing my wounded heart with all sorts of sin. But a feeling of guilt came over me, and I knew I needed to go to confession. I had so many embarrassing sins to tell this priest, who knew me, and I was very ashamed. But I went anyway. It was such a humbling experience. We sat face-to-face, and I told him my sins. I saved the one that I was most ashamed of until last. The priest wasn't angry with me like I thought he would be. Rather, he was like the loving father from the parable of the Prodigal Son. When I got it out, the priest said, "Ally, you've tasted real life. You can't go back to the counterfeit."

I did go back to the counterfeit; it was as if I couldn't walk away from the path of sin, even though I knew his words were true. And they continued to echo in my mind in moments of misery and despair—moments that, looking back, were kind of like the Prodigal Son eating out of a pig trough. God spoke to me through His priest. And eventually I accepted God's radical grace and returned to His loving embrace.

In the sacrament of Reconciliation, I have had moments of profound encounter with Jesus as well as seemingly ordinary encounters. But I have never been disappointed. He is there, the grace is there, and we are set free. If you were healed from cancer, wouldn't you just dance around the room? In this sacrament, our soul is healed, restored. It's something truly worth celebrating!

✳ ✳ ✳

In our journey with Christ, we are following Him—acting as He acts, thinking as He thinks, loving as He loves. The sacraments are means for our discipleship, food for our journey. The Eucharist is the bread of heaven, spiritual nourishment for our souls. And Reconciliation keeps us close to Christ as we fulfill our mission of loving God and other people.

PRACTICAL APPLICATION TO BECOME "DOERS OF THE WORD"

Prayerfully reflect on the areas of your life where you need the Lord to set you free from sin. Make time this week to go to the sacrament of Reconciliation. Rejoice in the Lord's unconditional love and forgiveness!

The next time you go to Mass, have expectancy that the Lord wants to speak to you. Listen for His voice through the Scriptures and in the silence of your heart after you receive the Eucharist.

Chapter 4

Forgiving One Another

Dave Nodar

"Forgiveness" has a nice ring to it; who's against forgiveness? But in reality forgiveness is hard. It goes against our instincts. I don't have a forgiving spirit when a driver on my left deliberately speeds up to keep me from shifting into his lane. But then I'm not especially generous when aggressive drivers want to pull in front of me either. I'm perfectly willing to receive forgiveness. But when I'm asked to forgive, well, I get pretty stiff-necked.

The disciples also had trouble with Jesus' teaching on forgiveness. Jesus often spoke about the importance of forgiveness. One example among many: "If you forgive men their trespasses, your heavenly Father also will forgive you; but if you do not forgive men their trespasses, neither will your Father forgive your trespasses" (Mt 6:14–15). The disciples naturally wondered how far this went. Many rabbis in Jesus' time had a three-strikes-and-you're-out rule; you would forgive someone three times, and then you could stop. So one day St. Peter went up to Jesus and asked "Lord, how often shall my brother sin against me, and I forgive him? As many as seven times?" (Mt 18:21).

St. Peter was asking a question we all ask. When do we stop forgiving the wayward spouse, the hostile in-law, the vindictive neighbor, the scheming coworker? Jesus gives St. Peter a hard answer. He answered, "I do not say to you seven times, but seventy times seven" (Mt 18:22). "Seventy times seven" is a reference to an infinitely large number. In other words, Jesus says we never stop forgiving.

That's a good thing, because the need for forgiveness is limitless. One of the tough lessons of life is that people in the world will hurt you. You meet them in school, in the workplace, in your communities. You might meet them in your family—neglectful parents, abusive spouses, angry siblings. You might find them kneeling next to you in church. My work in the ChristLife ministry has brought me wonderful relationships and lifelong friends, but I've also encountered people who deliberately set out to hurt me or my family and impede the work of the ministry.

At the same time, our mistakes, pride, ambition, and other faults hurt other people. We are all sinners. Alexander Solzhenitsyn, the great Russian writer, put it well in *The Gulag Archipelago*: "If only there were evil people somewhere insidiously committing evil deeds, and it were necessary only to separate them from the rest of us and destroy them! But the line dividing good and evil cuts through the heart of every human being. And who is willing to destroy a piece of his own heart?" We all need to forgive, and we all need forgiveness.

The consequences of not forgiving are terrible. We nurse grudges. Our minds replay slights and offenses in an endless loop of rancor. We fantasize about revenge. We grow bitter. Our personalities are blighted by resentment. I love the adage, "Resentment is like drinking poison and waiting for the other person to die."

Jesus offers us a way out. St. Paul told the Colossians, "He has delivered us from the dominion of darkness and transferred us to the kingdom of his beloved Son, in whom we have redemption, the forgiveness of sins" (Col 1:13–14). Christianity isn't just about thinking differently. It's about transformation. The Holy Spirit changes us from the inside out. The world is concerned with external appearances, but the Lord is concerned with our hearts. He wants to change hearts of stone into hearts full of love (cf. Ezek 36:26). This work begins when we're baptized, and the Lord has promised to finish it. As St. Paul said, "He who began a good work in you will bring it to completion at the day of Jesus Christ" (Phil 1:6).

JESUS CAME FOR FORGIVENESS

Repentance and forgiveness of sins are at the heart of the Gospel. The most solemn moment of Jesus' public ministry was the Last Supper, where He showed the apostles how He would remain with them and what they were to do to carry on His work. He gave them the Eucharist:

> He took a chalice, and when he had given thanks he gave it to them, saying, "Drink of it, all of you; for *this is my blood of the covenant, which is poured out for many for the forgiveness of sins.*" (Mt 26:27–28, emphasis added)

Before Jesus came, humanity was in deep trouble. Human beings were the apex of creation, the focus of God's love, yet we rebelled. We turned away from love and followed our own path—a path that led to discord, violence, misery, and estrangement from God. In His love, God reached out. He made a covenant with His chosen people. He sent prophets to speak His Word and formed kings to lead His people back to Him. God's people responded for a time, but always fell back into the old ways of sin. Finally, the Father sent His Son to take on Himself all the evil that poisoned the human heart. He died a horrible death on a cross, a pure and sinless victim of treachery and violence. He did it to restore us to God. Christ's death is about reconciliation. His blood was *poured out for many for the forgiveness of sins.*

On the day of Pentecost, St. Peter told the huge crowd of onlookers what they needed to do to join in this miracle of God: "Repent, and be baptized every one of you in the name of Jesus Christ for the forgiveness of your sins; and you shall receive the gift of the Holy Spirit" (Acts 2:38). This is what it means when we say that Christ died for our sins. We are hopelessly entangled in sin. Evil drags us down despite our best efforts. But Christ's death and resurrection shows us the way out. We have hope. We need to repent—turn our backs on the old way and embrace the kingdom of God. If we do this, the Holy Spirit will come and give us the power to live in freedom and love.

FORGIVING OTHERS

"Go and do likewise" (Lk 10:37), Jesus said after telling the parable of the Good Samaritan. Following Christ is all about doing likewise—doing what Jesus did, thinking as He thought, and loving as He loved. Nowhere is this more important than in the matter of forgiving others. Jesus poured out His blood for the forgiveness of sins. By His grace, we're to do the same.

To underline the point, Jesus tells a very tough parable. A king decided to settle accounts with His servants. One of these servants owed the king a very large amount, yet the king had mercy on him and forgave him the debt. However, the servant turned around and attacked another servant who owed him money. He refused to forgive the debt. When the king heard about this, he called the man back, revoked the pardon he had granted, and had him thrown into prison (Mt 18:23–35).

The lesson of the parable is very clear: Jesus insists that His servants have a forgiving spirit. It's a tough lesson. I know people who cannot say the words in the Our Father "forgive us our trespasses as we forgive those who trespass against us."

They cannot forgive others for the wrongs done to them. I sympathize with their pain. Many of the wounds people inflict on us are terrible injuries. Consider the abused child, the betrayed spouse, the person cheated by a business colleague or lied to by a treacherous friend. It seems very hard to forgive the people who do these things. Perhaps it is possible to be civil to them. Perhaps we can refrain from exacting revenge. But to forgive, really forgive? To forgive the way God forgives? That seems impossible.

But it is possible to forgive the way God forgives precisely because we are forgiven by Him. God does not forgive us because we deserve to be forgiven. We are not basically good people asking God to excuse infrequent slipups. We are sinners who are redeemed by a merciful, loving God, a God whose mercy knows no bounds. We can forgive those who have wounded us, not because they deserve to be forgiven, but because the grace of forgiveness empowers us. When Jesus commands us to forgive others in order to receive the Father's forgiveness, we can confidently expect His supernatural grace will make possible the impossible.

The most powerful moral values in the everyday world are fairness and justice. Anyone with small children knows this. Every piece of cake served to the kids must be perfectly equal. Wrongs must be righted. The guilty must be punished, and the punishment must be calibrated to fit the offense. This principle was enshrined in the old Law: an eye for an eye, a tooth for a tooth. But Jesus asks for something beyond fairness and justice.

> "You have heard that it was said, 'An eye for an eye and a tooth for a tooth.' But I say to you, Do not resist one who is evil. But if any one strikes you on the right cheek, turn to him the other also; and if anyone would sue you and take your coat, let him have your cloak as well; and if anyone forces

you to go one mile, go with him two miles." (Mt 5:38–41)

Forgiveness is a very radical teaching. We see how radical it is in situations of unfathomable evil. Some time ago, Muslim fanatics murdered fifty-eight Syrian Christians at Mass, including many children and babies. A survivor was asked what he would say to the murderers. He said, "We forgive you." A racist gunman murdered nine African-American Christians at a Bible study in South Carolina. Many members of the church forgave the killer and prayed that he would repent. Forgiveness in situations like these seems like an extraordinary thing—and it is. It's possible only through the grace of Jesus Christ. It's a wonderful gift. Our human instinct is to make someone pay for what they've done, but down that road lies an endless cycle of retaliation and revenge. Jesus instructs and empowers us for a new grace-filled way.

Hopefully, most of us will not be challenged to forgive in such tragic circumstances. But we all understand how difficult it can be. We all face circumstances when forgiveness is the exact opposite of what we feel like doing. We also know the consequences of not forgiving. We've all known the sour taste of the resentment and bitterness that takes over our hearts when we don't forgive.

Unforgiveness is spiritual poison. When we say, "I want justice, I want revenge, I'll never forget, I'll never forgive," we break off communion with God. Saying these things means we don't want to remain in His grace. We don't want to live in His kingdom, but we'll pitch our tent in a sad and lonely place where we nurse grudges, savor resentments, and punish everyone for their slights and failures and shortcomings. Jesus wants to lift us out of the state of separation from God and take us to a place of mercy. He says, "This is where you're going to find life. This is where you're going to find peace and power not only for your benefit but for the benefit of others."

HOW TO FORGIVE

The first step in cultivating a spirit of forgiveness is to take a long, hard, skeptical look at yourself. You are a wounded sinner, just like the people who anger you and make your life more difficult than you think it should be. You may be touchy, selfish, narrow-minded, or judgmental—just as you perceive them to be. A German Jew named Hela Ehrlich wrote a memoir recounting how she was freed of the bitterness that afflicted her because she was so angry at the Nazis who murdered her family and childhood friends. The breakthrough came when she understood that she too needed forgiveness:

> Trembling, I realized that if I looked into my own heart, I could find seeds of hatred there too. Arrogant thoughts, feelings of irritation toward others, coldness, anger, envy, and indifference. These are the roots of what happened in Nazi Germany. And they are in every human being. As I recognized more clearly than ever before that I myself stood in desperate need of forgiveness, I was able to forgive. And finally, I felt completely free. (Johann Christoph Arnold, *Why Forgive?*)

This kind of self-knowledge makes it easier to forgive others. When someone wounds us, we instinctively regard them through the very narrow lens of our pain. *They are spiteful, cruel, self-centered. They'll never change. This is how they are.* But if you know that you are weak and limited too, it's easier to extend to others the mercy you hope will be extended to you.

Awareness of our own shortcomings also tempers our harsh judgments of others. Is that hurtful remark a vicious attack on you, or was it simply an opinion that you didn't like? What's your part in the matter? Did someone say or do something that touched a sore spot, something you're embarrassed about? A few times in my life, I have been hurt by critical remarks about simple, mundane things and at times significant things. On reflection, I came to see that the pain was mainly in how I handled their comments. The criticism was sincere. I didn't like it, but it was just a critique.

To forgive, we need to surrender our "right" to get even. In Jesus, there is no right to hurt people who hurt us, although we like to think there is. One of the most poisonous aspects of resentment is the fantasy of revenge we indulge in when we're wounded. We relish pictures of terrible misfortunes befalling the person who said the nasty thing or snubbed us or passed us over for promotion. At the root of this is an urge to see people made to pay for what they've done. Jesus calls us to a different standard entirely. We are to look at the perfectly innocent victim on the cross, surrounded by a jeering crowd. And Jesus says, "Father forgive them, they don't know what they're doing."

Forgiveness is an act of the will. We've chosen to follow that man on the cross, Jesus. We want to imitate Him, be like Him, and do what He does. A big part of this package is saying, as He did, "Father forgive them." Often we must *choose* to do this, just as we chose to become Christians by an act of our will. Forgiveness is also an act of the will. It's a choice we make. We often must make it in the teeth of a great storm of wounded feelings and a voice in our heads shouting, "This isn't fair." The voice is often correct. What happened to us *may not be* fair. But our call is to be like Jesus. If we turn to Him in faith and obedience, He will give us the grace to forgive.

Don't wait for the other person to ask for forgiveness. It seems "only fair" to look for some acknowledgment of wrongdoing before you forgive someone, but in reality this attitude returns us to the "eye for an eye" principle of justice, which locks us into an endless cycle of accusation and recrimination. It's not enough to be willing to forgive people who are repentant. Christ calls us to forgive those who don't repent.

I don't want to minimize how difficult this can be. I'm sure the families of the Syrian Catholics murdered at Mass found it very difficult to forgive the killers. But think about the alternative. If you don't forgive because people don't ask for it, you're in a prison of pain and resentment. I've seen the consequences in many families. Brothers and sisters, parents and children are estranged for decades because of some offense that happened long ago. The reason for the breach might even be forgotten, yet family members have gotten used to thinking of each other as nasty, cold, and unworthy people whom you see only at funerals. Think about it in terms of your own peace and happiness and obedience to Jesus. Forgiveness drains bitterness away and sets your heart at rest. Refusing to forgive until someone repents turns control of your happiness over to someone else. By forgiving unconditionally, you walk out of the prison of animosity and walk into the grace of God.

Genuine forgiveness implies we can come to a place where we sincerely wish the best for people who have wounded us. This is another difficult challenge. It's often a long journey from a choice to forgive made out of obedience to Christ to a place where we genuinely rejoice when blessings come to people who have done us harm. But this is the place where Jesus will take us. The first step is to simply pray for the person. As Jesus said, "Pray for those who persecute you" (Mt 5:44).

There's a difference between forgiveness and reconciliation. Forgiveness brings you freedom, but it doesn't solve everything. Forgiveness is in your power; you can always forgive those who injure you. Reconciliation requires that the injured parties come together and resolve their differences. This isn't always possible. There will be situations where you won't be able to work things out. People who've wounded you will die, leaving unfinished business. There will always be troubles. "If it is possible, so far as it depends upon you, live peaceably with all," St. Paul wrote (Rom 12:18). A wise teaching—live peaceably *so far as it depends on you.* Much is out of our control. All the more reason to forgive freely when we can, pray for those who've hurt us, and work for peace constantly.

Forgiveness doesn't mean we have to put up with everything. We might continue to maintain difficult relationships and endure situations that are far from perfect, but forgiveness does not mean that we need to continue to suffer trauma and abuse. Sometimes it's necessary for children to be removed from abusive homes and spouses to leave abusive marriages. Sometimes we need to walk away from jobs (and bosses) that exploit us. Sometimes we must put distance between ourselves and the wounded, troubled, unhappy people in our lives. Sometimes, the harm that's done to us is a crime. We can forgive, but we might also need to alert authorities and cooperate in bringing people to legal justice.

Sometimes it's necessary to seek help for the effects of major trauma. Physical, emotional, and sexual abuse leave deep wounds that damage people in profound ways. Trained professionals can often be very helpful. It is always a bad idea to hide the experiences of major trauma. Bringing traumatic experiences into the light helps us receive God's healing grace. Obviously, we must carefully choose the people who will hear about our deepest pain.

One of the best things we can do to enjoy these graces is to get into the habit of asking for forgiveness. Do it explicitly. Don't just say, "I'm sorry if that offended you." Say something like, "Please forgive me for … showing up late for our lunch date … snapping at you just now … forgetting to call…." When someone asks you for forgiveness, give it freely. Forgiveness makes us one. It repairs breaches. It guards our unity. Practice it as often as you can, make it your lifestyle as Jesus' disciple.

PRACTICAL APPLICATION TO BECOME "DOERS OF THE WORD"

Think about a person or persons who have hurt you and ask the Lord for the grace to forgive them Take time to specifically identify by name and pray for each person you have unforgiveness toward. Pray the simple prayer below, choosing to forgive each person by name. Say the prayer aloud.

> *Father, I choose to forgive _____. I lay down my judgment at your cross. Lord Jesus, I give _____ a free gift of forgiveness. I forgive them just as you forgave me. I choose to live in the freedom Jesus has given me. Thank you, Father, for your mercy. Amen.*

Here is a list of people with whom you have relationships that you may need to forgive: parents, grandparents, siblings, other relatives, teachers, or pastors.

Chapter 5

The Spirit-Empowered Life

Dave Nodar

After they absorbed the shock and surprise of Jesus' resurrection, the disciples asked, "What now?" Would they go on as before, accompanying Jesus in His work of healing and teaching? Would they go off on their own? Jesus had trained them to go on missionary trips in pairs. What about the future? What plans did Jesus have to continue His work after they were gone? Maybe something unexpected would happen. "Lord, will you at this time restore the kingdom to Israel?" they asked (Acts 1:6).

Jesus told them it wasn't going to be a political restoration of Israel, and it wasn't going to be a continuation of His mission in the same manner. The same anointing of the Spirit that Jesus had received when He was baptized by John was now going to come on them. "You shall receive power when the Holy Spirit has come upon you; and you will be my witnesses in Jerusalem and in all Judea and Samaria and to the end of the earth" (Acts 1:8). Jesus told them to wait for this to happen, and then He left them as He ascended into heaven to be with the Father.

What happened next was nothing less than a complete transformation of the disciples. At Pentecost, the Holy Spirit came on them as Jesus promised and everything changed. The timid, confused disciples burst out into the streets of Jerusalem preaching the good news of the Gospel fearlessly. Even their speech was a miracle; all the foreigners in the city heard their preaching in their own language. Thousands of people responded to this message and changed their minds about who Jesus was. They repented of their sins, were baptized, and received the same power given to the disciples. The apostles went around the city healing the sick, casting out evil spirits, and raising the dead. The new believers formed communities. The Church was born.

It turned out that Jesus was not gone at all. He wasn't physically present anymore, but He was very much alive in the new Church through the power of the Holy Spirit. Jesus told the disciples, "It is to your advantage that I go away" (Jn 16:7). This was why. The Holy Spirit came in Jesus' place, igniting a wave of evangelism that spread the Gospel to all corners of the earth.

This same Holy Spirit comes to each of us when we are baptized and confirmed. Through the Spirit, Jesus is present to us all the time. The Spirit empowers us to think with His mind, see with His eyes, feel with His heart, and speak His words. We are able live a spirit-empowered life.

Years ago, I experienced a release of the Holy Spirit that was something like what the disciples must have experienced on Pentecost. I asked the Lord Jesus to come into my life and take over. I asked Him to be the center of my life and empower me with the Holy Spirit. I was transformed, just as the early Christians were and many Christians throughout the ages. I came to understand what it means to live a spirit-empowered life. The fruit of this encounter with the Holy Spirit was a hunger for prayer, Scripture, and the sacraments; a deep desire for fellowship with other Christians; and a joy in telling others about the love of God in Christ Jesus.

Asking Jesus to be the Lord and Savior our lives and for baptism in the Holy Spirit—making this decision of the will—is a renewal of our baptismal and confirmation promises. It releases the power of the Holy Spirit. This is key to living a Spirit-empowered life in Christ.

A NEW PENTECOST

Over the centuries, the Church has waxed and waned in her recognition of the Holy Spirit's importance in the lives of ordinary Christians. At times Catholics have been very cautious about the Spirit, saying the miracles and excitement and passion of Pentecost were things that happened in the early Church and not after. These times of neglect have been followed by periods of renewed emphasis on the gifts of the Spirit. We're living in a time of renewed emphasis.

In 1962, Pope St. John XXIII opened the Second Vatican Council for the purpose of renewing the Church's mission to evangelize the modern world. He asked the entire Church to pray for a new outpouring of the Holy Spirit: "Renew Your wonders in this day, as by a new Pentecost." Within a few years a Catholic charismatic movement began. Catholics throughout the world experienced the power of the Spirit changing their lives, a release of the charismatic gifts including tongues and prophecy, and an outpouring of fervor and joy in their faith. This swelled into a large movement of renewal that affected worship, personal evangelism, youth ministry, and empowerment for lay mission. Over 120 million Catholics have been part of the Catholic Charismatic renewal. The post–Vatican II years have also seen the emergence of other lay renewal movements bringing new energy in the mission of the Church.

Pope St. John Paul II saw all of this as an answer to Pope St. John XXIII's prayer for a new Pentecost. God had done something wonderful, he told a gathering of five hundred thousand people in Rome in 1998. "The Church rediscovered the charismatic dimension as one of her constitutive elements," he said. "Whenever the Spirit intervenes, He leaves people astonished. He brings about events of amazing newness. He radically changes persons and history." The Pope said the sacraments and the ministrations of the Church are not the only ways the Holy Spirit acts in us. The Spirit also gives us gifts that make us "fit and ready to undertake various tasks and offices for the renewal and building up of the Church."

I want us to take up this challenge of Pope St. John Paul II. We need to rediscover the charismatic dimension of our faith. Many of us have a good grasp on the importance of the sacraments. But most of us struggle in our understanding of life in the Spirit. We need to grow in openness to the Spirit's action that makes us holy and empowers us for mission.

CHILDREN OF GOD

One of the most precious gifts of the Holy Spirit is what St. Paul calls the spirit of adoption. "You have received a spirit of adoption. When we cry, 'Abba! Father!' it is that very Spirit bearing witness with our spirit that we are children of God" (Rom 8:15–16).

Here is the fundamental truth of being a Christian: we are sons and daughters of God. St. Paul explains, "If children, then heirs, heirs of God and fellow heirs with Christ, provided we suffer with him in order that we may also be glorified with him" (Rom 8:17). In other words, because we are God's adopted sons and daughters, we will inherit everything that He has—an eternal life in glory.

Many people feel alone and abandoned. This is the devastating tragedy of the human condition, one felt very acutely in this modern age of materialism and the destruction of family life. Separated from God, we are truly lost. We have no future and no hope. Relationships with others are fragile and fleeting. The Holy Spirit repairs this aching wound. "To all who received him, who believed in his name, he gave power to become children of God" (Jn 1:12).

It's impossible to exaggerate how important this is. The Holy Spirit puts us into the right relationship with God. It's not a relationship of fear or subservience. It's the relationship of Father and children. Children obey their father's commands, but they are also members of a great family with rights and status. Children are loved by their father. This was very personal for St. Paul, as he proclaimed that Christ "loved me and gave himself for me" (Gal 2:20). Suddenly an abstract theological idea became real, as it can for each of us. It changes the way we live, the way we think—it changes everything.

This was what I experienced when I was converted back in 1971. I suddenly knew God loved *me*—Dave, a confused, empty young man who now knew personally that he was loved! This was God's choice, not mine. I had nothing to do with it. I certainly didn't deserve it. I became a beloved son of God not because of anything I had done, but because of what Christ had done. The Holy Spirit brought this reality to me in a powerful way. I had simply said yes to Jesus as Lord and the Father's love for me was poured into my heart through the Holy Spirit who was given to me (see Rom 5:5)!

Knowing your identity as child of God is essential to the Christian life. If it is not yet a true part of who you are, ask the Holy Spirit to reveal the Father's personal love for you.

CHANGED INTO GOD'S LIKENESS

The Lord loves you just as you are—but He loves you so much that He won't leave you just as you are. The same Spirit who makes us children of God also changes us into people who are more and more like Jesus. "All, with unveiled face, beholding the glory of the Lord, are being changed into his likeness from one degree of glory to another," St. Paul writes (2 Cor 3:18). The theological word for it is "sanctified." Sanctified means being set apart, transformed from the inside out. We are part of God's family, and we gradually take on the family likeness through the work of the Spirit.

We grow in faith, hope, and love. Over time, as we cooperate with the Spirit, He produces fruit: love, joy, peace, patience, kindness, goodness, faithfulness, gentleness, and self-control (see Gal 5:22–23).

Being changed into God's likeness is an ongoing process. It's the work of the Spirit to which you say, "Yes, I want to be like Jesus." Stay close to the Lord, obey Him, and patiently allow the Spirit to do the work of interior transformation.

The community of faith we entered at Baptism becomes real and concrete as we grow in the Spirit. We find brothers and sisters with whom we can share our lives and together grow in holiness and mission.

WE'RE ON A MISSION FROM GOD

We are people on a mission. His work is to save people from sin, Satan, and eternal death. He described His mission at the beginning of His public ministry: "The Spirit of the Lord is upon me, because he has anointed me to preach good news to the poor. He has sent me to proclaim release to the captives and recovering of sight to the blind, to set at liberty those who are oppressed" (Lk 4:18). This mission continues, and He invites us to join Him in it.

The Church teaches there are two universal callings of every baptized Christian. They are holiness and evangelization. In others words, it is the Spirit who empowers you and me to be disciples on mission.

INSPIRATIONS IN DAILY LIFE

One of the key ways the Holy Spirit leads us on mission is in our ordinary daily circumstances. As you begin your day, ask the Lord to lead you and give you opportunities to bring heaven to earth for those you encounter. It may be as simple as a kind word in your family or to the gas station attendant. It may be an opportunity to meet regularly with a friend for coffee to read a book together that helps them to discover the meaning of life in our Lord. It may be striking up a conversation with a homeless person and offering him a sandwich. It could be an obvious departure from your schedule with what I call a divine appointment, where an opportunity to share how Jesus changed your life opens up.

Pope Francis talks about this dynamic: "Being a disciple means being constantly ready to bring the love of Jesus to others, and this can happen unexpectedly and in any place: on the street, in a city square, during work, on a journey" (*The Joy of the Gospel*, 127).

SPIRITUAL GIFTS

The Holy Spirit gives us the gifts we need to do His work. When the disciples received the Holy Spirit at Pentecost, they received spiritual gifts to carry out Christ's work of building the Church. We can receive them as well. They are gifts that empower us to confirm the truth of the Gospel and to serve others. Gifts are given to us for the sake of others.

The area of spiritual gifts may be something wholly new to you. My intention is to tell you that the use of these gifts is actually occurring for many Catholics and other Christians today. These gifts can help increase our effectiveness in evangelizing.

In the First Letter to the Corinthians, St. Paul writes, "Now concerning spiritual gifts, brethren, I do not want you to be uninformed" (1 Cor 12:1). Uninformed? No kidding. For a long time Catholics were completely uniformed about spiritual gifts. Passages in the New Testament explaining charismatic gifts were glossed over or explained away. One of the great contributions of the charismatic renewal is bringing new attention to what Scripture teaches about charismatic gifts. So let's take a look at how St. Paul informed the Corinthians about spiritual gifts.

> To each is given the manifestation of the Spirit for
> the common good. To one is given through the
> Spirit the utterance of wisdom, and to another
> the utterance of knowledge according to the
> same Spirit, to another faith by the same Spirit,
> to another gifts of healing by the one Spirit, to
> another the working of miracles, to another
> prophecy, to another the ability to distinguish
> between spirits, to another various kinds of
> tongues, to another the interpretation of tongues.
> All these are inspired by one and the same Spirit,
> who apportions to each one individually as he
> wills. (1 Cor 12:7–11)

This is not an exhaustive list. There are many other
spiritual gifts—compare also the lists in Romans 12:5–8;
Ephesians 4:11–12; 1 Peter 4: 9–11. Each gift is a manifestation
of the Lord's presence, given to us for the benefit of others.
Jesus and the disciples exercised these gifts. We can, too. The
Church teaches that these charisms are meant for us today.
The *Catechism* says: "Charisms are to be accepted with
gratitude by the person who receives them and by all members
of the Church as well. They are a wonderfully rich grace for
the apostolic vitality and for the holiness of the entire Body of
Christ" (CCC 800). Note that gifts of the Spirit are gifts freely
given, while fruit of the Spirit is grown over time. Gifts are not
based on our worth or holiness. They are given to us for the
sake of serving others and advancing the Gospel.

Some people aren't comfortable with spiritual gifts.
Things like prophecy, healing, and tongues don't fit inside the
comfortable box of habit and rationality we live in most of
the time.

One religious sister I know, who for many years had
been extremely resistant to the idea of spiritual gifts, had a
radical change of mind and conversion in her relationship to

the Lord Jesus. She began to earnestly desire the spiritual gifts in her life. When some of her friends heard about her change of mind, they were alarmed and asked why she was now open to them. She replied, "Have you read the Acts of the Apostles recently?" She went on to say, "We need all the spiritual gifts that God offers to the Church at this time in history!"

"Earnestly desire the spiritual gifts," St. Paul says (1 Cor 14:1). If they are gifts from God, shouldn't I desire and ask for them? According to the *Catechism*, they are given for the "apostolic vitality" of the Church today (CCC 800). We should be eager to have them so that we can respond to Christ's invitation to work with Him.

GIFTS FOR MISSION

In 1 Corinthians 12, St. Paul refers to knowledge, wisdom, prophecy, tongues, and the interpretation of tongues. These are called word gifts.

Prophecy, knowledge, and wisdom all involve the Holy Spirit revealing something to you for the sake of someone else. Often prophecy is presented as if the Lord were speaking in the first person; other times we simply share a sense of what we believe the Lord wants to say to someone.

Let me offer you a simple way to understand how the word gifts operate. Occasionally, as we are praying or reading Scripture, we experience a thought we know comes from God. "Be at peace," or "All will be well," or "I want you to change," or "Do not go down that road." When the Lord speaks in this way, we listen carefully and do our best to respond. In a similar way we may receive inspirations like this for the sake of others. We share it, for prophecy is intended to encourage, console, and build up others, as St. Paul teaches in 1 Corinthians 14:3.

Once during our daily office prayer, one of our staff read a Scripture verse out loud. She had a sense that the Lord wanted one of us to hear it. It was Zephaniah 3:15: "The LORD has taken away the judgments against you." At the time I was in the middle of a terrible bout of feeling awful about my past sins. I knew in my head God had forgiven me years ago, but my heart was tormented with guilt. When she spoke that verse, the Lord spoke directly to my heart. I felt His love and forgiveness. The oppression was lifted from me. My heart was reassured because that woman exercised the gift of prophecy through Scripture.

Here is another example of the word gifts. As I was preparing to speak at a large gathering, I distinctly had a word of knowledge come to me that there were two women with the same name sitting behind me in different areas of the room. I knew neither of them and had not yet seen them. The Holy Spirit revealed where they were sitting and gave me a word to encourage both of them. I spoke in front of the gathering, sharing that the Lord wanted them to not lose heart during the trials they were facing and to persevere in prayer knowing He was aware of their situations. The two ladies were very encouraged, and so were many others in the room who saw how intimately concerned God was for each of us.

Word gifts bring good news to other people. They can strengthen and encourage people, often in personal ways that allow them to know God loves them. Growing in prophecy requires practice. Being with others who are experienced in the gifts can help us to learn to exercise them. If you think you hear something for someone else, share it with them in a simple, humble manner. The Lord will help us grow in the use of the gifts if we do it in a gentle way, always open to the possibility that you may not get it right, yet with a willingness to step out and share it for the sake of others.

Another word gift is the gift of tongues. Tongues is primarily a prayer language that bypasses the intellect. It's the Holy Spirit praying with our spirit in a new language. It strengthens the one who is praying in tongues and is very useful for the sake of others. We don't understand this language ourselves, but God does. St. Paul says that one who speaks in tongues speaks not to men, but to God (1 Cor 14:2). What does it mean when St. Paul says we speak to God? Simply that the gift of tongues is a prayer language. Like the other gifts, tongues does not take over our emotions or vocal faculties. Normally, you hear some syllables in your mind and begin to speak them out. It often begins like a child uttering his first words and grows into more words as you exercise this gift. Usually people who desire this gift ask someone with the gift to pray with them to receive it.

The gift of tongues is invaluable for intercession. I pray for many people regularly. Sometimes I know how to pray for them, but sometimes I don't. I may not know what's going on in their lives. In times like these I often pray inaudibly in tongues. I may not know exactly how to pray for them, but the Spirit always does, so I pray in the Spirit's language.

The gift of tongues is also helpful when one is troubled and upset. One of my children was once in a life-threatening situation. I was terribly frightened and so upset that I found it hard to pray. I cried out to the Lord and began to pray in tongues. As I prayed, I experienced a sense of peace and the presence of the Lord despite my child's peril. I knew the Lord was aware of the situation and called me to trust Him. As it turned out, my child made it through the danger and the situation ended well.

The gift of tongues is also a gift of praise. Often when I'm thanking and praising God, I reach the limits of my vocabulary. No words of mine can adequately describe God's beauty and goodness and generosity. When I become especially aware of this, I'll sing or pray in tongues. It's a deeply satisfying way to pray.

Another spiritual gift particularly useful for the mission is the gift of healing. St. Paul speaks of this gift in First Corinthians 12:9. Jesus prayed for healing frequently, as did the disciples. The gift of healing isn't limited to the pages of the New Testament. It is very much alive today and has been throughout the history of the Church.

Healing is a sign of God's love. The healings Jesus performed revealed the truth of His words that the kingdom of God was at hand. Healings were signs of the rule of God breaking into our present world. They were physical demonstrations of the deeper healing Jesus was accomplishing—the healing of our separation from a loving Father. Jesus' saving work continues today.

I have witnessed genuine healings and have been used to pray for healings. Years ago my niece, Kate, fractured her wrist. An X-ray showed a severe fracture that would require surgery. A bone had chipped and had reversed from its correct position. My son and I prayed for her briefly. I placed my hand on her wrist and asked the Holy Spirit to heal it in Jesus' name. When she went back for a second X-ray to prepare for surgery, the bone had reversed into the proper position. She was healed, and the surgery was canceled! My son, Jake, said, "Dad, how did He do that?"

I look constantly for opportunities to pray for healing. Not everyone I pray for is healed—many aren't. But I tell everyone I pray for that God loves them. Some of the deepest spiritual conversations I've experienced were with people I prayed with but who weren't healed. They were moved simply by my offer to pray for them. I say, "God loves you and wants you to know that He's with you. Let me tell you more about the life He has for you."

Be open to the spiritual gifts. Desire them. Seek opportunities to grow in your understanding of them. The Christian life is intended to be one of joy, peace, and power in the Holy Spirit. It is good news not simply because we are on our way to heaven, but because we can bring heaven to earth for others. That is why we pray, "[Let] your kingdom come, [let] your will be done."

PRACTICAL APPLICATION TO BECOME "DOERS OF THE WORD"

Pray and ask the Holy Spirit to draw you into a deeper revelation of the Father's love for you. Pray that the Holy Spirit will grant you sensitivity to His inspirations during daily circumstances to share God's love with others.

In this chapter we have only scratched the surface regarding spiritual gifts. Entire books and seminars are dedicated to teaching and releasing the gifts. Try to find a place where you can receive teaching and practice the use of the gifts. "Make love your aim and earnestly desire the spiritual gifts" (1 Cor 14:1).

I recommend the book *Healing: Bringing the Gift of God's Mercy to the World* by Dr. Mary Healy (Our Sunday Visitor, 2015) to learn more about the spiritual gifts, especially healing.

Chapter 6

The World

Fr. Erik Arnold

> In the following three chapters ("The World," "The Flesh,"
> and "The Devil"), Dave, Ally, and I hope to prepare you
> for the struggles you will face as followers of Christ. It's
> important to be prepared when you embark on a new or
> renewed life as a Christian and to have a good grasp on the
> nature of these troubles. Where do they come from? How
> do they affect us? What can we do about them?

The weeks and months that followed my conversion at the end
of college were marked with intense joy and a tremendous
amount of grace. The Lord showered me with favors and daily
help that let my newly rediscovered Christian faith take root
in my life. Difficulties and struggles that I feared would be
impossible to overcome now seemed minuscule and small.

While I would have loved for things to have remained
that easy for years to come, the community of Christian friends
around me knew better. They were further along on their
spiritual journeys, and they let me know that the Christian
life always includes conflict and struggle. "Jesus never said this

was going to be an easy thing," they said. In fact, Jesus' own words—and His own life—made it clear that those who follow Him would have many troubles. I took these warnings to heart and tried to be as prepared as I could. I'm so thankful that my friends prepared me the way they did because our struggles in the spiritual life can be incredibly difficult at times. If we are not ready for them, we may be overwhelmed by discouragement and doubt, or even walk away.

In these next three chapters, Dave, Ally, and I hope to do for you what my friends did for me. It's important to be prepared for trouble when you embark on a new or renewed life as a Christian. It's important to have a good grasp on the nature of these troubles. Where do they come from? How do they affect us? What can we do about them? It's like the difference between being on a cruise ship or a battleship. People on a cruise ship are there to relax and have a good time. Their expectations would leave them surprised and distraught if the ship were to sail into a hurricane or come under attack. People on a battleship, on the other hand, know that they sail in troubled waters. When the enemy shows up, or when the storms come, they are ready.

DELIVERED FROM DARKNESS

The fact that the Christian life involves struggle is evident in the life of Christ Himself. Immediately after He was baptized by John, Jesus was assaulted by the devil in the desert. He resisted these temptations, began His public ministry, and was immediately thrust into conflict. The Pharisees, the Sadducees, and the Jewish elders opposed Him. Satan continued to stalk Him. His own disciples and family members misunderstood Him and sometimes opposed Him. He spent His time with people who were sick, possessed by demons, and desperately poor. He knew sin and its effects up close.

Jesus' world is our world. Living as a Christian means walking with Jesus into situations racked with conflict, pain, and failure. Jesus said it plainly: "If any man would come after me, let him deny himself and take up his cross and follow me"

(Mt 16:24). St. Paul cast the spiritual struggle in even starker terms, as a battle between two kingdoms: the dominion of darkness and the kingdom of God. Describing what Christ has done for us in the work of salvation, he says: "He has delivered us from the dominion of darkness and transferred us into the kingdom of his beloved Son, in whom we have redemption, the forgiveness of sins" (1 Col 1:13–14). Jesus took on our flesh and entered into the kingdom of darkness, in order to set us free and lead us into the kingdom of God. This may sound dramatic to some, but the struggle is real. Pope Francis, in a daily Mass homily on October 11, 2013, said: "On this point, there are no nuances. There is a battle, and a battle where salvation is at play, eternal salvation; eternal salvation of us all."

This is the reality we live in. Living as a Christian brings great joy but also more difficulties. As Christians, we will experience pain and sorrow as we look at the world around us through the new eyes of faith. Decisions that used to be easy become harder because we're aware of the lies and deceptions around us. Conflict is inescapable. Jesus came for a reason, and He invites us to work alongside Him. And what is this work? "The reason the Son of God appeared was to destroy the works of the devil" (1 Jn 3:8).

The spiritual battle and enemies we face get their traditional names from Scripture: the world, the flesh, and the devil. These come from a dense passage in St. Paul's letter to the Ephesians that is worth examining closely.

> And you he made alive, when you were dead through the trespasses and sins in which you once walked, following the course of this world, following the prince of the power of the air, the spirit that is now at work in the sons of disobedience. Among these we all once lived in the passions of our flesh, following the desires of body and mind, and so we were by nature children of wrath, like the rest of mankind. But God, who is rich in mercy, out of the great love with which

he loved us, even when we were dead through our trespasses, made us alive together with Christ (by grace you have been saved). (Eph 2:1–5)

St. Paul says that before we came to Christ, we lived in "this world," where Satan dwells. The world is deeply influenced by the devil. He is particularly mischievous in stirring up the "passions of our flesh." This is the trio of danger: the world, influenced by Satan; the devil, devoted to defeating those who love God; and our own flesh, whose weaknesses the evil one knows and exploits. They are tightly bound together in one system. It's a formidable foe, but we need not fear it. God has made us alive in Christ, and Christ is victorious.

WHAT IS "THE WORLD"?

It's important to understand precisely what "the world" is. Scripture uses the word in two different ways, one positive and one negative. In the positive sense, the Bible says of the world: "God saw everything that he had made, and behold, it was very good" (Gen 1:31). Creation is good. Christ Himself took on our flesh and shares in human life. What a testimony to the goodness of creation! God loved the world so much that He sent His Son into it. "God sent the Son into the world, not to condemn the world, but that the world might be saved through him" (Jn 3:17).

A couple of important points follow from this. First, withdrawing from the world is not an option, as desirable as that might seem. Christ is in the world, saving it and healing it; we are too because we are followers of Christ, doing His work. Condemning the world is not an option either. God loves the world, and so must we.

The second use of "the world" in Scripture is negative. There are many things in the world that are dangerous, corrupt, and twisted by sin. This is "the world" John was talking about when he wrote, "Do not love the world or the things in the world," and when he said, "We know that we are of God, and the whole world is in the power of the Evil One" (1 Jn 2:15; 5:19). The "world" in this negative sense is the system of relationships, ideas, and values that are opposed to the Lordship of Christ. It's the system that resists the Gospel, is offended by Christ, and pushes back against the kingdom of God. This is "the world" that makes trouble for us. We need to be aware of it and learn how to handle it.

THE BATTLE FOR THE MIND

In our struggle with the world, the battleground is our mind, our way of thinking. That might not seem like the most likely battlefield, but it is. Why? Because all behavior is based on belief. I think and believe certain things are true, and my behavior flows out of that way of thinking.

So if the enemy can change the way I think, by whispering lies to me in the world, then he can change the way I act. If I believe I will truly be happy only if I am rich, then I will probably spend my life trying to become rich. All behavior is based on belief.

In this chapter, I want to look at some of the lies the world tells us, lies that are ultimately aimed at separating us from God by changing the way we think and so changing the way we act.

LIE: CREATION IS AN END IN ITSELF

Our struggle with the world is governed by one master lie. The lie is that the many gifts and beautiful things of God's creation can be made into ends in themselves. The truth is that the good things in the world are gifts from God and are meant to point back to God. We are meant to use these things in order to love and serve God and neighbor. But the world tells us that we can have them for ourselves, as ends in themselves. We can use people for our own gratification. We can surround ourselves with shiny toys that will make others admire us. We can work hard so that we can be successful and gain power over others.

No wonder we have trouble with the world. As Christians, we believe that everything God created is meant to point us back to Him, to lead us closer to Him. But the world pushes us to take what is good and corrupt it, by cutting its ties to God and making it an end in itself, rather than a way to grow close to Christ. We can do this with money, food, work, sexuality, success, and countless other things. Usually these things are not bad in themselves; but when they are separated from God, they can end up leading us astray. From this one master lie, that creation is an end in itself, flows many other lies. Here are some of the biggest ones.

LIE: "IT'S ALL RELATIVE"

The world says that there is no fixed truth. When creation is cut off from God, then truth is relative—it depends on the cultural context, circumstances, and individual judgment. A particular perspective on life—Christianity, for example—has authority only for the people who choose to follow it. It has no authority or claim on anyone else. In fact, according to the relativistic point of view, any value system that claims universal authority must be resisted.

Relativism rejects the idea of universal moral norms. *I* decide what is good for me. If I think it's okay to lie and cheat to get ahead, that's right for me. If I want to have sex with anyone I'm attracted to, that's okay too. Relativism means that no one is in any position to say that such behavior is wrong. Shortly before he was elected pope, Benedict XVI warned that the world is "moving toward a dictatorship of relativism which does not recognize anything as certain and which has as its highest goal one's own ego and one's own desires." Benedict went on to describe the Christian alternative:

> We have a different goal: the Son of God, true man. He is the measure of true humanism. Being an "Adult" means having a faith which does not follow the waves of today's fashions or the

latest novelties. A faith which is deeply rooted in friendship with Christ is adult and mature. It is this friendship which opens us up to all that is good and gives us the knowledge to judge true from false and deceit from truth. (Homily, Mass for the Election of the Roman Pontiff, April 18, 2005)

It's easy to see why Christians are going to have conflict with a world governed by relativism. Christians and relativists look at the world in fundamentally different ways. As Christians, we don't think that the Gospel is true only for us; we think it's true for everybody. We think that living a life modeled on Jesus Christ and faithful to the teachings of the Church He founded is the best way for people to live. Relativists reject this idea. Naturally, they also reject the Church that teaches this idea. This is the source of the hostility to the Church we see in the media, cultural institutions, and wide swaths of government and education. According to them, Christians are not only wrong; they are dangerous because they threaten the world's cherished freedom to do whatever it wants.

It's a great challenge to be faithful to the Gospel while loving all persons and living in peace with our neighbors. "Be wise as serpents and innocent as doves," Jesus said (Mt 10:16).

LIE: "IT'S ALL ABOUT EXTERNALS"

Another great lie of the world is that your value and worth are determined by externals—what you do, what you have, and what you look like—not by who you are. What kind of job do you have? How much money do you make? How thin are you? How white are your teeth?

When we believe that our value and worth are determined by these externals, we can spend a lifetime chasing after them, trying to meet world's standards. And just when we think we've met them, they change and become ever more unattainable. This is by design. The world's standards are actually unachievable.

Why would the world place an unachievable standard before us? In order to create a constant market for the products they can sell us. If my teeth are never quite white enough, or I'm never quite thin enough, then I might be open to spending my money on something that just might help me reach that goal. And as soon as I do, the goal changes.

From this lie, that it's all about externals, flows another closely related lie: that things can make us happy. The more things the better. People who have big houses, huge wardrobes, the latest electronic gadgets, and large bank accounts are happier than people who don't have these things. "Stuff" is what matters.

The truth is that our dignity and value don't come from the outside, but from the inside. We have been made in God's own image and likeness. Our value and worth don't fluctuate like the stock market, dependent on our looks or bank accounts. God is unchanging, and so is our incredible dignity and worth. Learning to live this truth in everyday life can be a tremendous challenge, but the freedom and joy it brings is worth the effort.

LIE: "I NEED IT NOW"

One powerful message we hear countless times every day is that we should satisfy our desires and do so as quickly as possible. We're bombarded by seductive advertising messages and images telling us we can have whatever we want. "Have it your way." "Just do it." We're told to take it now. Why wait? You're not getting any younger. You have only one life to live. Enjoy life. Indulge your fantasies. If you don't have enough money, borrow it. Technology makes it all so much easier; almost everything you want is just a few mouse clicks away.

The lie, "I need it now," leads to a sense of entitlement. Not only is it *possible* to have what we want right now. We *deserve* to have it right now. It's *better* to have it now than to wait. The "I want it now" message erodes the self-control and discipline that's needed to acquire an education, enter into stable relationships, and meet the challenges that life throws at us. The "I want it now" message leads to bad decisions. We can convince ourselves that something we want is right for us—even that God wants it too—simply because we want it so much.

This lie wreaks great havoc on our thinking about sexuality and marriage. We're told that we should satisfy our sexual desires. Behavioral norms and taboos that restrain sexual expression are to be swept away. Sex is the basis for relationships. Marriage is about getting what you want. But this mentality is about as far away from the Christian ideal as it is possible to be. Scripture and the Church tell us that love is about sacrifice and self-giving. It's about seeking the good for others, not for yourself.

At first, a renewed Christian life, lived in the power of the Holy Spirit, might look like a long vacation on a cruise ship. Eventually we recognize that all is not sweetness and light; we're actually sailing on a battleship, heading into trouble. Soon enough the battle is engaged. Let's look around the ship and take stock. What weapons do we have to fight this battle?

FORTIFIED BY TRUTH

First and foremost, our lives are based on the truth of Jesus Christ. Through Scripture and the teaching of the Church He reveals the true purpose of human life and guides us in the best way to live it. The world has it wrong. Life is not about money, sex, power, and success. A life based on satisfying one's desires leads to ruin, not joy. The truth isn't what seems good to each individual. Jesus Christ is the way, the truth, and the life. A life of fulfillment and joy lies in striving to be like Jesus and following His way.

It's important to recognize that we have truth on our side. Jesus said, "You will know the truth, and the truth will make you free" (Jn 8:32). The world doesn't believe this, it is threatened by truth and those who profess to know it. In a thousand ways, large and small, the world will try to undermine our commitment to the truth.

Our weapon in this struggle is our faith, which opens the door to the truth. Faith keeps us rooted in the truth and leads to victory. "Who is it that overcomes the world but he who believes that Jesus is the Son of God?" (1 Jn 5:5).

Remember that the battle is for our mind. St. Paul wrote, "Do not be conformed to this world but be transformed by the renewal of your mind, that you may prove what is the will of God, what is good and acceptable and perfect" (Rom 12:2). St. Paul writes about a process—being "transformed by the *renewal* of your mind." Our minds have to be constantly renewed in the truth, the truth of who God is and the truth of who we are. When we recognize lies that we have believed, the best spiritual remedy is to renounce them and embrace the truth of God. We will discuss more about renouncing lies in the chapter on the devil. This renewal of our minds is a lifelong task. We need to be in a place where we can learn the ways of God at all times.

A COMMUNITY OF FAITH

This place is the Church, the community of faith established by Christ to teach the ways of God and carry out His work in the world. We absolutely need the Church. We need to be in an environment where we can hear the truth and live it out with the encouragement and help of our brothers and sisters. The community of faith is not a place to flee to in order to escape the world. It's a place where the seed of our faith can take root and grow and flourish. The world is dry sand. Our faith won't grow there; it will wither and die. The Church is rich soil.

One of the most important ways our faith is nourished is through personal relationships with others who are striving to live as we are. I know the importance of this firsthand. After my conversion I became part of a community of young adults in my home parish, and I wouldn't be the kind of Christian I am today without them. They guided me, protected me, steered me in the right direction, and stood by me when hard times came. Christian relationships teach us and show us what the kingdom of God is like and our faith can't grow without them.

A PLACE TO LEARN AND THE POWER TO LIVE IT OUT

The Church is the primary place where we get good, sound teaching about living as a Christian in the world. Jesus said to His disciples, "He who hears you hears me" (Lk 10:16). Jesus still speaks to us through His Church. We can draw on the Church's vast wisdom through books, websites, videos, and other Catholic media. The Church has been engaged in struggle with the world for two thousand years. Many Catholics in the past have dealt with the problems we are facing. We're not alone. Through Scripture and the Magisterium the Lord is still guiding us. And when joined with the sacraments, we are given the grace and power to put into practice the truths we are learning. Thank goodness we are not left to rely on our own strength to make it happen!

IN THE WORLD BUT NOT OF IT

It's crucial to see that we are not trying to flee the world. To the contrary, we have a mission to the world. Jesus expresses this vital truth through several images. We are "the light of the world" and "a city built on a hill" meant to attract others (Mt 5:14). We are the "salt of the earth" (Mt 5:13). We are a mustard seed that grows into a great tree (see Mt 13:31–32). We are a small measure of yeast that eventually permeates the whole loaf (see Mt 13:33). You've got to be in the dough to affect the dough. You've got to be in the world if your light is going to shine on it. At the same time we need to be skeptical about the messages the world sends, knowing that it's not all true, and so be shielded from its destructive influences.

Jesus spoke of His followers' relationship to the world in His final prayer for His disciples. "They are not of the world, even as I am not of the world," He said to the Father (Jn 17:16). But He also said, "As you sent me into the world, so I have sent them into the world" (Jn 17:18). We need to be *in* the world but not *of* the world. This isn't an easy position to be in. We're in this world, but we're not at home here. We need to love, understand, and be with people in the world, recognizing that our values, goals, and ways of thinking may differ from theirs in important ways. We have been sent by the Lord to offer a witness in our lifestyle and words to true life that is only found in Him.

We can do this. It's not easy, but Christ makes it possible. He put us here, and His grace allows us to flourish here.

PRACTICAL APPLICATION TO BECOME "DOERS OF THE WORD"

Reflect on areas of the world's lies discussed in this chapter and note areas you recognize need to change in your thinking. Write these areas down and consider practical steps to renew your worldview to be conformed to Jesus' teaching.

Chapter 7

The Flesh

Ally Ascosi

When you start living a renewed life in the Spirit, it doesn't take long to recognize the problems posed by the world. Lots of people don't think the way you do. You recognize that you're on a battleship, not a cruise ship, as Fr. Erik puts it. You're sailing in troubled waters, and you'd better get ready for a fight.

"The world" is an external enemy. But there's another one—an enemy that lies within us. Our hearts are divided. Part of us wants God and the things of God; part of us wants nothing to do with God. It resists God. It wants power, glory, pleasure, and a thousand other things. It can be very unsettling to recognize this rebellion in our hearts. The world is one thing, it's "out there"—but this inner enemy, it's about *us*. As we dive into this chapter, we will need humility to take a good look at our inner struggle, but we are in this together.

After surrendering my life to Christ during my junior year of college, I was confused by this rebellion that was still inside of me. I had been renewed in the Holy Spirit; I received deep inner healing; I experienced new joy and freedom in my faith in Christ. Why, then, did part of me still push God away? Why did I feel a tug to return to my old way of life, where I was miserable and depressed? It made no sense. The Apostle Paul was confronted with the same thing: "I do not understand my own actions. For I do not do what I want, but I do the very thing I hate" (Rom 7:15).

THE SPIRIT AND THE FLESH

The traditional name for this inner enemy is "the flesh." Actually, in Scripture, "flesh" has two meanings just as "the world" does. The first meaning is our humanity created and loved by God. This is the meaning of flesh in Psalm 84:

> My soul longs, yes, it faints
> for the courts of the LORD;
> my heart and my flesh sing for joy
> to the living God. (Ps 84:2)

God created our humanity and all that goes with it with dignity, including our desires and drives. Christ shares this humanity. "And the Word became flesh" (Jn 1:14). In this sense our flesh is sanctified.

The other meaning of flesh is our sinful human nature. It's the twisting and misdirecting of the desires that God created as good. It's that part of us that resists God. It seeks to get what it wants, and sometimes our fleshly desires can seem irresistible. St. Paul says this:

> Do not gratify the desires of the flesh. For the desires of the flesh are against the Spirit, and the desires of the Spirit are against the flesh. (Gal 5:16–17)

There's a battle going on in our inmost being. The Spirit and the flesh are at odds. They pull in different directions. They want different things. There's no escaping this struggle. Note that St. Paul is writing to Christians who have *already* been baptized (and filled with the Holy Spirit). They are followers of Christ, yet they continue to battle the urges of the flesh. So it is with us. There will never be a cease-fire in the war with the flesh. The Spirit and the flesh will never sit down and negotiate a truce.

However, the redemption of our fallen natures has already been accomplished. If we surrender our lives to Jesus Christ, even though the struggle inside of us continues, we know who will win.

SINS OF THE FLESH

When we think of sins of the flesh, we usually think first of sexual sins. But sins of the flesh encompass more than sex. Consider the many works of the flesh listed by St. Paul in his letters to the Galatians and Colossians:

> Now the works of the flesh are plain: immorality, impurity, licentiousness, idolatry, sorcery, enmity, strife, jealousy, anger, selfishness, dissension, party spirit, envy, drunkenness, carousing, and the like. (Gal 5:19–21)

> Put to death therefore what is earthly in you: immorality, impurity, passion, evil desire, and covetousness, which is idolatry … anger, wrath, malice, slander, and foul talk from your mouth. (Col 3:5, 8)

When I first read these lists I thought that I was in pretty good shape. I'm a happily married woman living a respectable life. I'm not into sorcery and orgies, and I didn't even know what licentiousness was. But then I took a look at how these passages were rendered in the *The Message*, a modern-language paraphrase of Scripture:

> Repetitive, loveless, cheap sex … frenzied and joyless grabs for happiness … paranoid loneliness; cutthroat competition; all-consuming-yet-never-

satisfied wants; a brutal temper; an impotence to love or be loved; divided homes and divided lives … uncontrolled and uncontrollable addictions. (Gal 5:19–21, MSG)

Doing whatever you feel like whenever you feel like it, and grabbing whatever attracts your fancy … irritability … profanity, dirty talk. (Col 3:5–8, MSG)

Wow! This list really hit home for me: *Doing whatever you feel like whenever you feel like it*? Sleeping in instead of waking up to pray, browsing Pinterest instead reading Scripture, even taking a nap instead of taking care of the needs of my family; whatever I want. Even when I don't follow through on those urges, doing whatever I want can seem like a nice way to live. But really it's not; it's an enticement from the flesh that leaves us feeling empty. *A brutal temper?* Yup! Early in my marriage, my husband, Peter, and I were told that marriage is hard. But honestly, it didn't seem so bad, we rarely had arguments or issues with one another, I thought we were doing pretty well. But six years and four babies later, a simple discussion can get blown out of proportion very quickly. Lack of sleep, and a sound track of crying and whining in the background, can cause temper to well up in me that I didn't know existed.

Let me mention a couple of other sins of the flesh that aren't in these Scriptures. Doubt, for example. Some degree of doubt will always be with us this side of heaven. There will be times when we walk in darkness and pain, longing for an experience of the God we cannot see. But there is a kind of doubt that springs from a dark place. This is the doubt that denies that God exists, welcomes a universe without meaning, and scorns believers as fools. Another sin of the flesh is judgment. We're instantly critical of other people, looking for their failures and faults, and, of course, finding ourselves superior to them. There's a compulsive quality to sins of the flesh, a sense that "this is the way I am and I can't do anything about it." A good example is a seemingly small fault like grumpiness in the morning. "I didn't sleep well, I'm in a bad mood—stay away from me, don't talk to me." This is the flesh talking. If you give in to it, you can ruin the day for yourself and anyone else who has the misfortune to live with you.

A terrible and very common sin of the flesh is gossip. Gossip seems harmless (or at least not so very bad). Our world is full of celebrity gossip, political gossip, gossip about coworkers and people in our parish. Recently Peter and I had dinner with some neighbors whom we didn't know very well. We wanted to make a good impression and have great conversation. But what did we talk about? Our other neighbors! We didn't want to gossip, but it was too easy. In the middle of this I said to myself, "This isn't right; I shouldn't be doing this," but kept right on gossiping. It was a vivid experience of St. Paul's anguished cry: "I do not do what I want, but I do the very thing I hate" (Rom 7:15).

THE ROLE OF THE FLESH

Let's look at the role of the flesh in the broader conflict we face with the world and the devil (more on him in the next chapter). The flesh plays a particular role in this battle. It's our enemy within, working to undermine the defenses from the inside. In the Spanish Civil War in the 1930s, the Loyalist armies under General Franco launched an assault against the city of Madrid. Franco attacked in four columns, one from each direction. When asked which column would finally break through, Franco said, "The fifth column." By "the fifth column," Franco meant the people inside the city of Madrid who supported him. They told the city's defenders that resistance was futile. They sabotaged the defenses. They told people in the city that they would be better off under Franco. They promoted surrender. Sure enough, the city's defenses swiftly collapsed when the military columns attacked from the outside. The subversive fifth column was the decisive factor.

That's the role the flesh plays in our spiritual lives. The influences of the world and the devil that assault us are working on a fortress that isn't unified. The fifth column within is sending messages of doubt and sympathy with the enemy. "It wouldn't be so very bad to indulge myself a little bit here." "A lot of people you respect will think it's strange if you do that." Then comes the big lie: "You can't resist this; you're going to give into it anyway so you might as well do it now."

We sometimes get nostalgic for the free and easy life we lived before getting serious about being a Christian, a life that never existed. Look at the story in the book of Numbers about the Hebrew people in the desert. They had been slaves in Egypt, oppressed, beaten, scorned. God delivered them, but as soon as they met some difficulty in the desert they began to long for Egypt (see Num 11:5). Remember the fish we used to eat? Remember the melons? Remember how good we had it? This always puzzles me. Are they serious? Who cares about melons; they were slaves! But if we are honest with ourselves, we often let our appetites—our flesh—do the talking too.

On the other hand, a different life can look very attractive when the life you are actually living seems sad and unfulfilling. This can be a spur to make constructive changes, but the flesh can twist these longings into bad choices. This happened to me. I went to college as a serious Christian. I was firm in my faith for about a year. I was on the swim team, and we were encouraged to "bond" with our teammates. Most of the team bonding activities had to do with partying—"carousing," as St. Paul puts it. Initially, I avoided this; it didn't fit my Christian way of life. After sitting alone in my dorm room weekend after weekend, my desire to be included grew stronger.

So at the end of the swim season, I went to my first party. I didn't drink, but at least I wasn't sitting alone in my room. I began receiving a lot of attention, making friends, and finally feeling included. And soon I was going to lots of parties. And the sin in my life just escalated. I began drinking. Then came drugs and a whole lot of other things that are on St. Paul's lists of sins of the flesh. The friendships I made were superficial, and I ended up feeling more alone than I was before. I wound up in a very bad place. I kept a journal through this time. There are many entries about how miserable I was, without hope and without alternatives. But now it has become a beautiful documentation of the moments that led to my conversion back to God.

The day came when I looked at myself in the mirror and said, "Who are you?" I committed to stop drinking. I began making small steps toward God. Two days later I went to a prayer meeting. That night I wrote about my struggle to have a relationship with God in my journal: "I don't get it. I wonder if I ever got it. I don't even know what 'it' is." It's pretty sad, but I didn't really know God anymore. Two years earlier I had become Catholic and was living my life for Him, but now I forgot everything. My understanding was completely darkened, that's what sin does. Ten days later I wrote, "I want my life to be different. I think I want a personal relationship with you and all that jazz [yes, that's what I really wrote], but it's really hard for me, maybe you could change my heart." That was the opening God needed. I took one step toward God, and then I found myself running toward Him. I found the grace to open up my hard, dark heart and let God into it. I gave God a little bit, and He rushed in and took everything. In reading my journal, I realized that I had an overnight conversion. Things changed very fast. It was a beautiful experience of the reality of grace.

BY GRACE YOU HAVE BEEN SAVED

What happened to me can happen to you too. That's because Christ has triumphed over sin. The Spirit can overcome any work of the flesh that you're struggling with. You're not alone. God sent His Son clothed in our flesh to redeem it and set

us free so that we can walk in the Spirit and not in the flesh.
Here's how St. Paul puts it:

> God has done what the law, weakened by the
> flesh, could not do: sending his own Son in the
> likeness of sinful flesh and for sin, he condemned
> sin in the flesh, in order that the just requirement
> of the law might be fulfilled in us, who walk not
> according to the flesh but according to the Spirit.
> (Rom 8:3–4)

Note that last sentence. We "walk not according to the
flesh but according to the Spirit." This is good news—the best
news! We walk in the Spirit. We're not on our own in this
life, with all its pitfalls and challenges. We're not alone in our
battle with the flesh. The Holy Spirit gives us the courage and
patience and power we need to battle the world. The Spirit
does the same thing in our struggles with the flesh.

"By grace you have been saved," says St. Paul in
Ephesians. He wants to make sure we know this, so he says
it again: "By grace you have been saved through faith." And
then he draws out a very important implication of this fact:
"This is not your own doing; it is the gift of God—not because
of works" (Eph 2:5, 8). *This is not your own doing.* We've been
saved by grace; we don't deserve it. The power of the Spirit
within us will help us; all we have to do is yield to it.

Yielding doesn't come easily. By nature we're willpower
people. We find out what the rules are and do our best to follow
them: be kind to strangers, floss every day, don't eat cookies
at lunch, and call your mother. Willpower and following the
rules can take us a long way, but soon enough we'll meet the
enemy within—our flesh, rebelling against God, pushing us
off the path of freedom and into bondage. When this happens,
we need to yield to the power of the Spirit, remembering that
by grace we have been saved.

HOW TO BATTLE THE FLESH

That's the first step in battling the flesh—simply yielding control to the Holy Spirit. This is often harder than it sounds. In fact, a determination to keep control of our lives is one of the works of the flesh. The flesh resists the Spirit, and this is where it starts—at the very beginning, when Christ asks us to surrender to Him and allow the Spirit to do His work.

Another necessary attitude is obedience. The Spirit will tell you what you need to do to resist the flesh. When you hear Him, do what He says. Often, a gentle voice of conscience will speak up when you've set out to gossip or judge somebody or indulge some feelings of resentment or envy. That's the Spirit speaking. When we were gossiping about our neighbors at that dinner party, the thought crossed my mind that what we were doing was wrong. That was the Spirit telling me what to do. Sometimes you'll feel a little check in your spirit about something seemingly innocent and inconsequential. It might be a movie or TV show, or a friendship that doesn't seem quite right. For example, Peter and I have decided to limit our use of the TV, the Internet, and social media, to create space for more focused time with one another and our family.

An important breakthrough for me came when I dealt with stubborn unforgiveness toward my biological father. He had left the family when I was young and had done real harm to my mother, sister, and me. I didn't want to forgive him for what he did. Good friends told me that I was justified, I didn't have to forgive a man who had done terrible things and hadn't repented of them. But harboring this bitterness in my heart did me a lot of harm. It was hard for me to trust God. I was plagued by fears. It complicated my relationships with men. For a long time a feeling grew in me that there was something wrong about my attitude toward my father. Finally, I acted on this gentle prodding of the Spirit. When I forgave my father, I experienced a new freedom and peace. The love of Christ offered me a way out of the prison of resentment.

Another weapon in the battle against the flesh is knowledge of yourself. When you know your weaknesses, you're better able to anticipate trouble and defend yourself when the attack comes. I'm an introvert by nature. This is a strength when it comes to spending time alone in prayer and reflection. It's a weakness when it veers into self-pity and brooding. I battle this tendency by deliberately cultivating gratitude. Every day, I intentionally thank the Lord for the good things in my life. And Peter often challenges me, when I start to seem grumpy or in a sour mood, to share with him one thing (or sometimes five things) that I am thankful for.

It's wise to be proactive in those areas where you know you're weak. Regularly review the areas of your life that have given you trouble in the past. Mount your defenses. If you're inclined to self-pity, make a gratitude list. If you worry about money too much, give some away. If you have resentment concerning someone, pray for them and do something nice for them.

As time goes on, you will become more aware of the inner battle with the flesh. It is important to recognize that as Christians we are not exempt from the desires of the flesh. The very fact that we are engaged in a battle against the flesh points to the Holy Spirit's presence within us. St. Catherine of Siena, a consecrated nun and Doctor of the Church, was once severely tempted to sins of impurity. She fought them successfully, but, during a subsequent dialogue with Jesus in a vision, asked where He had been during the temptation:

> "Where were you, my dear Lord, when my heart was full of darkness and filth?" And He answered: I was within your heart, my daughter." "And how," she replied, "could you dwell within my heart which was full of impurities? Do you abide then in such unclean places?" And the Lord said to her: "Tell me, did these impure thoughts of your

heart cause you pleasure or sadness, bitterness or delight?" "Extreme bitterness and sadness," she replied. And He answered her, "Who was it that caused this great bitterness and sadness in your heart? It was myself, who remained hidden within the depths of your spirit." (*Introduction to the Devout Life*, IV, 4)

Like St. Catherine of Siena, as you grow in the Christian life you will begin to find the desires of the flesh less and less attractive, even to the point that they utterly repel you. This is proof that the Spirit of God is at work in your heart.

HELP FROM OTHERS

The community of our brothers and sisters gives invaluable help in this battle with the flesh. You're not an only child. You're part of God's family; you're surrounded by brothers and sisters. All of them are there to help you.

God's family is a fellowship of wounded healers. We all suffer; we all take our bumps in the battle with the world, the flesh, and the devil. We learn from this and use this experience to help someone else. I battled depression for several years. After I came out of it I wanted to forget about this bleak time in my life. But in the year after I recovered, four people with serious depression problems came to me for help. I was able to help them simply by sharing my experience. My friends listened to me because I understood what depression was like. I knew what it felt like to have a black cloud of hopelessness descend on you for no particular reason. I knew how annoying it was when friends say to cheer up and be happy when nothing you've tried makes you feel better. I also knew what it felt like to recover from depression. My suffering was the reason I was able to give other people hope.

One of our enemy's greatest tactics is fear of exposure, which encourages us to keep things in the dark. When we are able to talk about our sins of the flesh, they lose their power. Most importantly, go to the sacrament of Reconciliation! But don't underestimate having accountability from a friend or a small group in your faith community. James says, "Confess your sins to one another, and pray for one another, that you may be healed" (Jas 5:16). Things rot in the dark. They just become more and more shameful, but speaking it out loud—along with prayer for one another—brings freedom. For example, I have two close friends with whom I can freely talk about the ups and downs of life. We challenge one another to grow in holiness, and pray for one another. Together our vulnerability and honesty with one another have been instrumental in our spiritual growth.

FINAL ENCOURAGEMENT

Our struggle with the flesh requires patience. There will setbacks. There will be times that every step forward seems to be followed by two steps back. Some problems never seem to change. Victory requires persistent effort. Recall Jesus' parable of the sower who threw seed on rocks, among weeds, and onto good soil. Jesus said, "And as for that in the good soil, they are those who, hearing the word, hold it fast in an honest and good heart, and bring forth fruit *with patience*" (Lk 8:15).

We need to be patient, but also rejoice and give thanks. I often joke with people and say: "Do you want to know what God's will is for your life?" And they enthusiastically respond, "Sure!" Then I share this Scripture: "Rejoice always, pray constantly, give thanks in all circumstances; *for this is the will of God* in Christ Jesus for you" (1 Thess 5:16–18). He wants us to be thankful, because it's the key to our holiness. We rejoice always because "we know that in everything God works for good with those who love him, who are called according to his purpose" (Rom 8:28). We *know* these things, St. Paul says. The victory is already won. That's reason enough to rejoice.

So, yes, the flesh is still within us, but if we surrender our lives to Jesus Christ, it no longer has the same power over us. We are no longer slaves to our flesh. I've heard it said that the flesh and our spirit are like two wolves inside of us and they are warring, fighting. Which one will win? Whichever one you feed. And so let us commit to feeding our spirit, and the flesh will become weaker and weaker and we will continue to grow in holiness, imitating our Savior Jesus Christ.

PRACTICAL APPLICATION TO BECOME "DOERS OF THE WORD"

We reviewed the Scripture passages from Colossians and Galatians (including the modern paraphrase) earlier in the chapter that identify the works of the flesh. Meditate on those passages. Which sins of the flesh do you struggle with? Take time to pray to God, surrendering your life to Him and asking for His grace to help you overcome these areas of sin. If you have a journal, consider writing out your thoughts as a prayer to God.

If it has been a while, or you are struggling with serious sin, go to the sacrament of Reconciliation and receive the forgiveness of the Lord.

Seek out a friend or mentor with whom you can discuss your struggles with the desires of the flesh. Ask him or her to pray with you for strength to overcome these areas of sin.

Chapter 8

The Devil

Dave Nodar

When we follow Christ, we follow Him into trouble. Some of this trouble comes from the world—the network of social norms, cultural assumptions, and distorted values that oppose the Lordship of Jesus. Much of it comes from the flesh—the part of us corrupted by original sin that resists the freedom of the Gospel. These difficulties don't arise at random. There's a guiding source behind them that is designing a strategy to turn us away from Christ. This source is the devil. He's not a comic figure with a pitchfork and red tights. The devil is real.

A few minutes of exposure to the daily news feed gives plenty of evidence for the presence of a malignant, evil force at work in the world. The world is full of horror, suffering, and cruelty. Much of it makes no sense. People do evil for the fun of it, simply because they can. They do bad things that are contrary to their own best interests. They call evil good and good evil. Social institutions become corrupt and dangerous.

Yet people doubt the devil's existence. The secular mentality so influential in our culture does not allow for belief in the devil. There are even many Christians who do not believe in the devil. People might refer vaguely to a "dark side" or a "shadow self," but have nothing but scorn for those who speak of a personal evil intelligence at loose in the world. Occasionally, horrors like the 9/11 terrorist attacks and the random acts of violence in our cities might cause second thoughts about the reality of the devil, but usually not for long.

The Church, however, doesn't have any doubts about Satan. The *Catechism* says: "Behind the disobedient choice of our first parents lurks a seductive voice, opposed to God, which makes them fall into death out of envy (cf. *Gen* 3:1–5; *Wis* 2:24). Scripture and the Church's Tradition see in this being a fallen angel, called 'Satan' or the 'devil' (cf. *Jn* 8:44; *Rev* 12:9)" (CCC 391). Pope Francis speaks clearly about the battle we face against the devil: "Jesus came to destroy the devil, to give us the freedom from the enslavement the devil has over us. And this is not exaggerating. On this point, there are no nuances. There is a battle and a battle where salvation is at play, eternal salvation; [the] eternal salvation of us all" (Vatican Radio, Oct. 11, 2013). The battle against the devil is real, and as Christians it begins by knowing our enemy.

KNOWING OUR ENEMY

What is this enemy like? First and foremost, he is a liar. "When he lies, he speaks according to his own nature, for he is a liar and the father of lies," says Jesus (Jn 8:44). One of our most precious gifts from the Lord is truth. We have knowledge of the true nature of things. Through the Holy Spirit we have insight into realities hidden from others. Satan will do whatever he can to loosen our grasp of the truth. He will whisper sweet lies to tempt us into rebellion.

Satan is a murderer. "He was a murderer from the beginning," Jesus says (Jn 8:44). He is the enemy of life in all its forms. Satan wants to snuff out the life of the Spirit in us. He wants to close the door to eternal life. He is the author of wars and insurrections, abortions, and other violence that extinguish human life. Jesus said, "I came that they may have life, and have it abundantly" (Jn 10:10). The devil comes to bring death.

Satan is a malicious thief. "The thief comes only to steal and kill and destroy," says Jesus (Jn 10:10). He wants to take what we have—friendship with God, the life of the Spirit, the freedom of the Gospel. He is offended and threatened by our joy and freedom.

The devil accuses us. The word "Satan" means accuser. He is the corrupt witness telling lies about us and to us. He tells us we are terrible sinners who have done unforgivable things. He is the voice in our head saying that we don't deserve to be loved, that people would hate us if they knew the truth about us, that nothing is going to change, that it's not worth fighting off that persistent temptation because we're bound to give into it eventually. In the Book of Revelation, the victorious Lord says, "The accuser of our brethren has been thrown down" (Rev 12:10).

Satan is "the deceiver of the whole world" (Rev 12:9). He tries to keep us ignorant of the true nature of things. You might recall the movie *The Matrix*, in which the human race is beguiled by a fantasy disguising the fact that humans have been enslaved by dark powers. The devil operates the same way. He wants to keep us in the dark. He doesn't want us thinking about life after death. He doesn't want us to know that we're in a war.

Satan works to isolate us. He tries to separate us from friends, family, and the community of faith. He wants us to be alone, brooding about our sins, while our hope is melting away. One of his most effective lies many of us have struggled with—at one time or another—is that our sins and struggles are unique, no one can understand us, and no one has ever suffered the same way we suffer. The truth is that "no temptation has overtaken you that is not common to man" (1 Cor 10:13).

Satan is clever and shrewd. "Satan disguises himself as an angel of light" (2 Cor 11:14). His lies come wrapped in an attractive package. One obvious example is sexuality.

Sex is one of God's great gifts to us, but it is misused in a thousand ways. Sexual sin is a corruption of something that God created as good. Virtually all sin is like this. Satan takes something good and twists it out of shape. Something good is bent to evil ends.

Satan's goal is to take you out of the battle. If he can lure you into sin, you'll feel shame and guilt. You'll feel isolated from your Christian friends whom you imagine to be much "holier" than you. If all goes according to Satan's plan, you will isolate yourself in shame. You won't ask for help. You won't talk to anyone about it. You will fall deeper into sin. Eventually you'll see yourself as a hopeless sinner, and you'll give up. You'll cease to play your important role in Christ's work of saving and healing the world.

As a result we end up becoming "lukewarm" Christians. The Lord has harsh words for them: "Because you are lukewarm, and neither cold nor hot, I will spew you out of my mouth" (Rev 3:16). These words can be applied to Christians who are "spectators." They're out of the game, sitting on the sidelines. Christians in the battle can't count on them; Satan doesn't have to worry about them. They've been neutralized by the deceiver, the accuser, the prince of lies. In fact, what happens when we live a lukewarm existence is that we give an antiwitness to true life in Christ.

WEAK POINTS

You are like a stronghold, a castle on a hill subject to attacks. Satan is like the chief of a gang of bandits, circling the castle, looking for weak points. Or, to update the metaphor, you are an important website containing vital information. Satan is the leader of a gang of clever hackers, looking for a way in so he can steal what you have. You get the point: it's wise to find out where you are vulnerable and take steps to bolster your defenses.

One weak point for almost everyone is your thoughts. "As the serpent deceived Eve by his cunning, your thoughts will be led astray from a sincere and pure devotion to Christ," St. Paul told the Corinthians (2 Cor 11:3). Stand back from yourself for a moment and observe the stream of thoughts that pass in and out of your consciousness as the day goes on. A remarkable number of these thoughts are negative: frustration about your work; awareness of bodily discomfort; cynicism about what people say; misgivings; fears; irritations; an overall feeling of angst and boredom. They trigger anxiety and depression. They offer Satan a rich field for mischief—and worse.

We can defend ourselves by fighting to get control of this stream of negative thoughts. This is what St. Paul meant when he told the Corinthians to "take every thought captive to obey Christ" (2 Cor 10:5). Cultivate a spirit of gratitude. When you sense yourself slipping into negativity, stop and give thanks to the Lord. This doesn't mean you're putting on a pair of rose-colored glasses to hide the painful realities of life. To the contrary, it's a matter of seeing the truth that's hidden by negativity—the truth that we are sons and daughters of God, doing God's work in the world through the power of the Holy Spirit. Turn things around by magnifying and praising the Lord who is greater than any thoughts we encounter. When we exalt Him, it puts things in proper perspective and allows His grace to assist us in the battle for our mind.

As you do this, you will become skilled at detecting the enemy's voice. The enemy is the accuser. He condemns. He blames. He stirs up guilt and hopelessness. He tries to convince you nothing will ever change. Sometimes he will adopt a softer tone, switching from accusations to lies. He will stir up illusions and dreams in your imagination. He will suggest new projects that will make you wealthy, powerful, and famous. Countering the enemy's voice is the voice of the Holy Spirit. The Spirit never condemns. He never lies. The Spirit will draw your attention to areas of your life that need to change, but He will always do this in a constructive way, full of hope and confidence in the future.

As you look for weak points in your defenses, pay close attention to those areas that have been attacked before. These are the habitual sins you've struggled with for a while—sins of speech like gossip and slander; lust, gluttony, and other sins of the flesh; anger, impatience, and other sins that damage your relationships. Some weak points are not so much sins as areas of vulnerability. You might have a tendency to spend money too freely, for example, or you might know you're a sucker for any project that makes you look good to others.

Pay special attention to wounds from childhood. Many of us grow up in unstable families that don't provide the emotional security necessary for healthy development. Sadly, many children are the victims of physical, sexual, and emotional abuse that leave lasting wounds. Even if we think our family was "normal," we might come into adulthood with anxieties and weaknesses rooted in childhood. These problems are typically long lasting. We need to be aware of how they affect us.

Traumas in life often open up weak points where the enemy can gain a foothold. Common life events like the untimely death of a loved one, serious illness, and financial problems can make it difficult to carry on normal life. They can cause great trouble in our spiritual lives. I experienced this first-hand a number of years ago when I went through a divorce. It was a terrible time. The enemy used this misfortune to attack me. *How could this happen to someone who has been serving God so faithfully? Maybe God doesn't love you as much as you thought He did. Maybe there's something seriously wrong with you.* And, eventually, he whispered: *A divorced man shouldn't be in a ministry like this. You should quit and do something else.*

Satan works in irrational impulses and strange thoughts. You're driving down the road and suddenly think about driving into a telephone pole. You might have a notion to attack a person who offends you. Lustful thoughts come out of nowhere and grip your imagination. You're sitting at your desk, working or studying as usual, and suddenly think that what you're doing is useless and meaningless. Thoughts like these are common. We seldom act on them, but they are troublesome and distracting. This is the enemy, blowing smoke in your eyes, distracting you, causing trouble, and softening you up for another attack somewhere else.

Quite often, the attack has something to do with unity. Jesus prayed that we would all be one. Satan would love to see us divided and alone—isolated individuals mistrusting each other, instead of a unified body. Disunity is everywhere. Recently I wanted to find out what the popes have taught about the devil. I put the question in a search engine and came up with dozens of web pages written by non-Catholic Christians accusing Catholics of being devil worshippers. You don't have to look hard to find other examples. Catholics fear and mistrust other Catholics. Parishes are divided. The enemy attacks the unity of families. While driving to church on a Sunday morning, suddenly the kids start fighting in the car, or spouses begin arguing. When things like this happen, treat it as an attack on our unity.

Finally, avoid anything that has to do with the occult. Many people, especially young people, experiment with Tarot cards, Ouija boards, fortune-tellers, charms, and other occult paraphernalia, thinking it's harmless fun. But it isn't harmless. These practices summon evil spiritual forces and bring them into our lives. They provide a wide-open door for Satan to wreak havoc. Get rid of occult paraphernalia. If you have been involved in occult practices, go to confession and ask for prayer, because it is a sure thing that the evil one will use this area to attack you.

LIVING IN THE TRUTH

Satan is the prince of lies. Our best defense against him is to live in the truth. Pilate, one of Satan's servants, cynically asked Jesus, "What is truth?" (Jn 18:38). Earlier in John's Gospel, Jesus gave the answer: "I am the way, and the truth, and the life" (Jn 14:6). In other words, truth is a Person. We know the truth by knowing Jesus. This is the cornerstone of our strategy to combat Satan.

Do everything you can to know Jesus better. Hang out with Jesus. Make personal prayer a priority. Read the Gospels. Take time for Eucharistic Adoration. Talk to Him when you get some downtime. Turn off the radio when you're in the car and spend time praising and thanking Him for the blessings in your life. When you do these things, you are living in the truth. Satan can't live there. Jesus said, "If you continue in my word, you are truly my disciples, and you will know the truth, and the truth will make you free" (Jn 8:31–32). That's a remarkable promise. Take time to memorize Scripture verses that renew the way you think about God, yourself, and others. Take advantage of Christ's promises by getting to know Jesus as well as you can. When you are anxious about the many things you have to do, stop for a moment and pray. Whenever your spirit is disturbed and you sense that you're slipping into nervous worry, stop and reconnect with Jesus.

Living in the truth means holding fast to the truth of who we are: sons and daughters of God, heirs to the riches of the Kingdom. John writes, "See what love the Father has given us, that we should be called children of God; and so we are" (1 Jn 3:1). Not surprisingly, the devil likes to attack us in our fundamental identity. He will sow doubt and mistrust. His goal is to separate us from the Father, Son, and Spirit.

Satan succeeded spectacularly well with this strategy at the beginning of the human story. He tempted Eve by causing her to doubt that her connection to God was as close as she thought it was. "Did God *really* tell you not to eat from the trees?" he asked. "No, just this one tree," Eve said. "Why?" Satan asked. "Because we'll die if we eat it," she responded. "Oh, no, you won't die," Satan said. "If you eat it you'll be like God, and He doesn't want any rivals." Satan's lies challenged Eve's identity as a daughter of God. She began to doubt that God was telling her the truth. She began to like the idea that she was a powerful, autonomous individual, capable of great things only after she freed herself from the shackles of obedience to God. The devil employs the same strategy against us. He will attack you in your fundamental identity as a son or daughter of God. This is why it is so important to remain anchored in the truth of the Person of Jesus Christ.

THE LORD'S TRIUMPH

There's one very important thing to know about Satan: he's a loser. He was defeated by the Cross. His power was broken, and his ultimate defeat is just a matter of time. This means that in any given temptation or battle, the Lord is always more powerful than Satan. No temptation is irresistible. No addiction is too strong to be broken. No obsession is so deep you can't escape it. There is always hope. When you're deep in hand-to-hand combat with the enemy, you can always call on the name of Jesus Christ, and help will come.

Even though Satan has lost the war, the fighting continues. Our position is like that of soldiers fighting in the last year or so of World War II. The allied invasion of Europe on D-Day sealed Hitler's fate. Nazi Germany was destined to lose the war. Nothing could reverse that inevitable outcome, but bloody fighting continued for some months. The Allies took casualties and suffered setbacks. So it is with us. We know Christ is victorious, but the fight goes on until the Lord's return in glory.

It's important to remember we are on the winning side. "He who is in you is greater than he who is in the world" (1 Jn 4:4). "He has delivered us from the dominion of darkness and transferred us to the kingdom of his beloved Son" (Col 1:13). Memorize these verses. Pray over them. Write them on a piece of paper and put it on your bathroom mirror so it's the first thing you see in the morning and the last thing you see at night. Say these verses when you are battling the flesh—a persistent temptation, an irrational urge, a decline into doubt and despair. Say them when you feel afraid. Say them when your life overflows with problems that don't have an obvious solution. You have access to a power that's greater than anything life can throw at you—the power of Jesus Christ.

PRACTICAL APPLICATION TO BECOME "DOERS OF THE WORD"

Introduction

This two-step practical application invites you to renew your baptismal promises and to renounce specific areas influenced by the devil. It is important to speak the following statements and prayers out loud for several reasons:

1. The spoken word has power. It reveals the heart.
2. When we invoke the name of Jesus, we speak with His authority. It is a privilege to speak in the name of Jesus. To speak His name means to speak His character and in His authority, in union with His Spirit. When we say, "I forgive or renounce in the name of Jesus," these words have the power to bring about what they signify.
3. Demons cannot read our minds. It is not good enough to think, "I renounce this or that." When they hear the words, they know that their power is broken.

Renewal of Baptismal Promises

When we renew our baptismal promises, we consciously reject the influence of the devil and sin in our lives, and we declare our belief in the Holy Trinity and the fundamental truths of our faith. The following baptismal renewal has been adjusted for personal use:

> *I reject sin so I may live in freedom as a [son or daughter] of God.*
>
> *I reject the glamor of evil and refuse to be mastered by sin.*
>
> *I reject Satan, the father of sin and prince of darkness.*
>
> *I believe in God, the Father Almighty, creator of heaven and earth.*
>
> *I believe in Jesus Christ, His only Son, our Lord, who was born of the Virgin Mary, was crucified, died, and was buried, rose from the dead, and is now seated at the right hand of the Father.*
>
> *I believe in the Holy Spirit, the holy Catholic Church, the communion of saints, the forgiveness of sins, the resurrection of the body, and life everlasting. Amen!*

Renouncing Specific Areas

After reading this chapter, you may have identified specific areas of possible influence of evil spirits; areas where the devil may have a foothold; areas where you are vulnerable to the devil's influence; areas where you want to be free.

Here are some areas that may be influenced by evil spirits: pride, anger, envy, fear, lust, doubt, self-righteousness, abandonment, depression, marital infidelity, slander, impurity, gossip, judgment, control, self sufficiency, disunity, occult practices, insecurity, hatred, and/or addiction (food, alcohol, drugs, gambling, pornography).

Opening prayer

> *Father I want to be free from the influence of the devil in all areas of my life. Send Your Holy Spirit to help identify the areas in my life where I need to be free. Give me the courage to turn from these areas and turn toward You.*

Statement of renunciation [repeat for each specific area where you desire freedom]:

> *In the name of Jesus I renounce a spirit of _____ .*

Closing prayer

> *Thank you, Lord Jesus, for giving me freedom and authority over my enemies. Fill me with Your perfect love and peace. Amen.*

Remember, "He who is in you is greater than he who is in the world" (1 John 4:4). What you just did is real. It has power.

FURTHER READING

Resisting the Devil: A Catholic Perspective on Deliverance, Neal Lozano (Our Sunday Visitor, 2010).

Unbound: A Practical Guide to Deliverance, Neal Lozano (Chosen Books, 2010).

Chapter 9

Advancing the Mission of the Church

Dave Nodar

The Lord has blessed us so abundantly that we can scarcely comprehend it. He has brought us out of darkness and into the light of grace and love. He has filled us with His Holy Spirit to renew and guide us. He has given us brothers and sisters with whom we can share our lives. He has shown us who God is—a God of love, pouring out His blessings in an endless stream of grace. We were lost, but now we are found. "The LORD has done great things for us," sings the Psalmist (Ps 126:3).

You see, these blessings are not meant only for ourselves. We are called to share them with others. The Lord calls us in two ways when we welcome His love into our lives and respond to His call. The first is a call to be holy. We are set apart from the world, transformed by the power of the Spirit, empowered by His grace to live lives worthy of Christ. We are called to be saints. So far, this book has provided guidance in how to do that. But there's a second universal call. We're called to participate in the essential mission of the Church—the Great Commission—which is to evangelize the world. The Lord asks us to engage people in our world and help them come to know the saving

113

love of Christ. Each one of us has an important part in this work. We are not complete as Christians until we discover how we are called to share Christ's love with others.

You might be tempted to wonder how you can respond to the Lord's call to mission in your own life. You look at the news, or just take a long look at the pain and suffering in the lives of people around you, and think, "How can I possibly make a difference in this?" Well, you *can* make a difference. People just like you have made a difference since the beginning of the Church. The Lord does the work. He has changed entire cultures. And He does it by working through ordinary Christians like you who surrender their lives to Him and ask Him to use their talents for His work. Often it may seem like what we're doing is something small, but if we are responding to the Holy Spirit, and yielding to Him, He can use us in significant ways.

One story from the Acts of the Apostles makes the point. The disciples created a great uproar in Jerusalem after they received the Holy Spirit at Pentecost. They preached boldly and performed miracles, which brought people to Christ by the thousands. This made the religious and civil authorities angry. They hauled St. Peter and St. John before them and demanded an explanation. After listening to Peter give a fervent declaration that Jesus rose from the dead and was Lord and Messiah, the authorities noticed that Peter and John "were uneducated, common men" (Acts 4:13). We think of the apostles as extraordinary leaders with remarkable talents, but that's not how they appeared to people around them. They were normal guys who didn't seem capable of doing what they were doing.

The Jerusalem authorities recognized that Peter and John had been with Jesus (see Acts 4:13). That is the key. The Lord can use us as we continue to draw closer to Him with confidence in His love. The Lord does the work; we are His instruments, tools in His hands. We're useful to the extent that we are close to Him and attentive to His leading.

THE CALL TO THE LAITY

The Church was born on Pentecost when the Holy Spirit came down on the disciples in dramatic fashion. The disciples immediately went into the streets proclaiming the Gospel to anyone who would listen. This is the paradigm for understanding the mission of the Church. The disciples didn't retreat into the desert to form a pure Church untainted by the world. They didn't huddle in strategy sessions to figure out how to navigate the tricky political situation they were in. They didn't even seem to spend much time reflecting on the meaning of the life, death, and resurrection of Jesus. All those things (and many others) eventually came. But the essential impulse was to fulfill the Lord's command to take the Gospel to the nations.

This still is the mission of the Church. The Decree on the Apostolate of the Laity (*Apostolicam Actuositatem*) says so plainly:

> The Church was founded for the purpose of spreading the kingdom of Christ throughout the earth for the glory of God the Father, to enable all men to share in His saving redemption, and that through them the whole world might enter into a relationship with Christ. (2)

In this document, Bl. Pope Paul VI explains that everything the Church does to spread the kingdom of Christ is the apostolate. Furthermore, every Christian is called to be part of it: "On all Christians therefore is laid the preeminent responsibility of working to make the divine message of salvation known and accepted by all men throughout the world" (*Apostolicam Actuositatem*, 3).

The Church recognizes three vocations: bishops, priests, and laity. The work of evangelizing the world is especially the responsibility of the laity. The Decree continues: "The apostolate of the laity derives from their Christian vocation and the Church can never be without it … in fact, modern conditions demand that their apostolate be broadened and intensified" (*Apostolicam Actuositatem*, 1).

Recent popes have stressed the importance of intensifying the involvement of the laity in the mission of the Church. Some reasons are practical, such as the shortage of priests making it ever more necessary for laypeople to be active in mission. But the main reason is that evangelization is the proper role for the laity.

ORDINARY PEOPLE

The Acts of the Apostles describes a couple of people whom we can look to as models of evangelization. Both are ordinary people—new Christians who emerged to do great things.

The first is St. Stephen. You can read his story in Acts 6 and 7. St. Stephen emerged to prominence as a result of the early Church's first "manpower crisis." The Apostles were stretched to the limit, and a task that became neglected was the care of widows in the community. Widows were vulnerable because they had no husbands to take care of them, so the community itself took on the responsibility of caring for them. The apostles decided to give this responsibility to some men in the community. St. Stephen, "a man full of faith and the Holy Spirit" (Acts 6:5), was tapped for the job of caring for these poor and vulnerable. (It's worth pointing out that the apostles chose six other men to do this work, too.) Evidently, caring for the poor was a big job in the early Church just as it is today.

In addition, St. Stephen manifested many spiritual gifts. Signs and wonders accompanied his proclamation of the Gospel, and there was great power in his preaching and debate. St. Stephen's place in the Church's history is a glorious one. He was killed by a mob enraged by his preaching, becoming the Church's first martyr.

The second person is a woman named Tabitha who lived in the town of Joppa. She is described as a "disciple," who was "full of good works and acts of charity" (Acts 9:36). She spent her life serving. Sadly, Tabitha falls ill and dies. Her friends immediately ask Peter to come. This wasn't simply a request that St. Peter come to her funeral. They were hoping Peter would be able to do something about her death. Note their very high expectations of what the Lord could do through His disciple. Peter came to the room where Tabitha was laid out. He prayed, received direction from the Lord, and ordered her to rise. She opened her eyes and stood up. She was resurrected from the dead. News of the remarkable miracle spread like wildfire, and many came to faith in the Lord as a result.

Tabitha and Stephen gave witness to the Lord both in life and death. In life they were devoted to good works. Their deaths were occasions for more glory to God. That's what we want for ourselves. We should desire to serve God in both life and death. And we should give serious thought to serving the poor and needy as they did. Pope Francis has called on Christians to give direct personal service to the poor. Don't just write a check to charities (though that is important, too). Connect with needy people personally.

My friends Pete and Ally do exactly that. Pete and Ally are a young couple with small children and a very busy life, yet they make time to reach out to people in need. One of their friends is a young single woman with a small child. They met her when she was pregnant and alone, with few friends and limited resources. They've helped in many ways, but their greatest gift to her is their personal love and care.

My friend Larry makes huge, splendid dinners for various Church events. He buys the food and organizes a team to cook and serve it. He's done this for his parish, for a Catholic girls' school, for ChristLife, and other groups. Larry is not a professional chef, but he likes to cook, and he obviously has a flair for organization.

Peter and Ally have a gift for friendship. Larry has a gift for cooking on a grand scale. What are your gifts? Pray about them. Ask the Lord how you should use them for His work. Ask the Holy Spirit to direct you.

THE ADULTERESS AND THE TAXMAN

Anyone can become an evangelist. You don't have to be eloquent, uniquely talented, or "holy." Sinners with a sketchy past can introduce people to Christ's love. All you have to do is talk to others about the way God has loved you.

The Decree on the Apostolate of the Laity says that we are "apostles"—the word means "one who is sent." What do apostles do? The Decree says: "A true apostle looks for opportunities to announce Christ by words addressed either to non-believers with a view of leading them to the faith or, to the faithful, with a view of instructing, strengthening, and encouraging them to a more fervent life" (*Apostolicam Actuositatem*, 6).

We have many opportunities to do that. Many people in our culture desperately need to hear the good news of the Gospel. They know very little about the Christian message. They live in a culture dominated by pagan values. They are searching for meaning. They are burdened with troubles. They don't know that God is inviting them to a life of peace and joy. Someone needs to tell them. Why can't it be you?

Consider the anonymous Samaritan woman in John 4. She's living with a man who is not her husband, and she had five husbands before that. She's a public sinner shunned by her neighbors. She has to draw water from the village well in the middle of the day, when it is the hottest, instead of morning and evening when "respectable" women come to the well. She's sitting there in the hot sun when Jesus comes by with several of His disciples. Jesus speaks to her (to the disciples' dismay).

He speaks to her about her life. He tells her about living water, about true worship, and about the Messiah.

The astonished woman gets up, runs into town, and tells the people about the prophet who knew everything about her. The people invite Jesus to stay with them, and He spends two days teaching them. Many are converted because of the sinful woman transformed into an evangelist through the love of Christ.

Another example is one of my favorite evangelizers, Zacchaeus, the tax collector, whose story is told in Luke 19. Zacchaeus had become rich collecting taxes for the Roman overlords. He lived in Jericho, an affluent town, and when Jesus came to town, he came out to see what all the fuss was about. What happened next is slightly comical. Zacchaeus was a short man—he was height challenged! He couldn't see Jesus because the crowd was in the way. We can imagine little Zacchaeus running around behind the crowd, trying to elbow his way to the front. The people wouldn't give him a break. They despised tax collectors and shoved him back with snarls and curses. So Zacchaeus climbed a tree to get a better view. This was something a boy might do, but it was certainly not something a rich man would do. Zacchaeus did it anyway because he needed to see Jesus.

Jesus spotted him in the tree and called out: "Zacchaeus, make haste and come down; for I must stay at your house today" (Lk 19:5). The people who saw this were aghast: "He has gone to be the guest of a man who is a sinner" (Lk 19:7). But Jesus explained that Zacchaeus was a son of Abraham just as they were. Jesus belonged in his house. Jesus' mission was "to seek out and to save the lost" (Lk 19:10). Zacchaeus responds to Jesus' invitation with an act of extraordinary generosity. He wants nothing more than to follow Jesus, the Messiah. He gave half of his possessions to the poor. He vowed to repay anyone he defrauded four times the amount he stole. Hearing this, Jesus said, "Today salvation has come to this house" (Lk 19:9).

Zacchaeus was a changed man, converted to the cause of Christ, and the proof of his conversion had to do with what was most important to him: money. He did what the rich young man in Matthew 19 wouldn't do: sell his possessions, give the money to the poor, and follow Jesus. Jesus talks about money often, almost always to warn us about the spiritual dangers it presents. Money distracts us from what's important. It lures us into a way of life that's bad for us. He told a chilling parable about a rich man who kept building more barns to store his grain and goods. The man could be a commendable American capitalist working industriously to build his business and make more money. Then he suddenly dies one night. All his wealth is meaningless. All the time he spent acquiring it is wasted. Jesus calls him a fool.

Jesus regarded money very differently than we do. For Him, money has spiritual significance. It does great spiritual harm if we place too much importance on it. But it does great spiritual good if we use it properly, as Zacchaeus did after this conversion. In contrast, many of us tend to separate money and our spirituality. We do what we have to do to make a living. We spend what money we have to spend to live like our neighbors do (and maybe a little bit better than they do). We buy things we don't really need simply because we want them. None of this seems to affect our spiritual lives very much. We believe our spiritual lives have to do with spiritual things, not material things. This is what the rich fool thought.

Jesus wants our heart. He said, "Where your treasure is, there your heart will be also" (Mt 6:21). Our treasure is where we spend our time, energy, and, also our money. It's important that we take a long, hard look at these things. For many of us, that means looking at how much money we spend for the Kingdom of God. How generous are you, really?

A GENEROUS LIFESTYLE

Generosity begins with gratitude. Consider King David's marvelous prayer of gratitude in 1 Chronicles 29. He listed the generous offerings the people made for the building of the temple: gold and silver, precious jewels, bronze, onyx, marble, fine wood—the wealth of the nation, all given to build a beautiful place where God could dwell. But all this wealth, David said, is God's gift.

> Who am I, and what is my people, that we should be able thus to offer willingly? For all things come from you, and of your own have we given you. For we are strangers before you, and sojourners, as all our fathers were; our days on the earth are like a shadow, and there is no abiding. O LORD our God, all this abundance that we have provided for building you a house for your holy name comes from your hand and is all your own. (1 Chron 29:14–16)

David recognizes something important: everything we are and everything we have belongs to God because it comes from God. When we give our treasure for the work of the Church, we are only returning to God what is already His. The idea that our money is *ours* is an illusion. God gives it to us. We are only taking care of it for a while. It belongs to Him, and we dispose of it according to His will.

The New Testament sets forth a two-fold perspective on money: generosity and freedom. We're to be generous, giving abundantly out of love. We're also to give freely, not under the law as slaves. We are sons and daughters of the King enjoying the riches of the Kingdom. St. Paul tells us, "God loves a cheerful giver" (2 Cor 9:7). The economy of the Kingdom is different than the economy of the world. We keep what we have by giving it away. As we give, we receive. "God is able to provide you with every blessing in abundance, so that you may always have enough of everything and may provide in abundance for every good work" (2 Cor 9:8).

Most of us have some work to do in this department. Many Christians live a lifestyle indistinguishable from everyone else. The fruit of Catholic generosity is all around us; a great network of parishes, schools, charitable organizations, and ministries has been built and supported by generous givers. But many Catholics don't give very much at all today.

The scriptural attitude about giving essentially says that the first fruits of what we have belong to God. This is the *best* of what we have: the best animals, the best part of the harvest, the best part of the day, the best use of our talents and gifts. In the Old Testament and in Jesus' time, this "first fruits" attitude is expressed as the expectation that people give a tithe—that is, 10 percent—of what they have to the Church. I think this is a good guideline for us. Consider building a 10 percent tithe right into your budget. I follow an approach suggested by a bishop; I give 5 percent of my income to my parish and 5 percent to other ministries and charities. I regard it as my responsibility; "The faithful are obliged to assist with the material needs of the Church, each according to his own ability" (CCC 2043).

I've known many people who tithe from their income. Many of them are not people of means. I think of my friends Adrian and Therese. They have seven children, and Adrian works as a maintenance man at a university. They always tithe and keep money around for people in need. And they always have what they need. Yes, they live simply—but that's the point. They live the way they do because they are Christians. We want to live a lifestyle that reflects we are followers of Christ.

MARY OUR MODEL

The Decree on the Apostolate of the Laity holds Mary as the great model for apostles of Christ. Her entire life was one of submission and devotion to the Lord. She told the servants at the wedding feast at Cana, "Do whatever he tells you" (Jn 2:5). She tells us the same thing. The work of saving and healing the world is Christ's work. He invites us to join Him and take on the role each of us has in this great missionary adventure. Get close to Him and do whatever He tells you.

Mary did this perfectly. The Decree points out that Mary lived an ordinary human life "filled with family concerns and labors" (4). But she was intimately united with her Son. She was attentive to Him, and she cooperated with Him. Now she is poised to help us do the same:

> Having now been assumed into heaven, with her maternal charity she cares for these brothers of her Son who are still on their earthly pilgrimage and remain involved in dangers and difficulties until they are led into the happy fatherland. All should devoutly venerate her and commend their life and apostolate to her maternal care. (*Apostolicam Actuositatem*, 4)

Reflect on Mary's example. Ask her intercession for the work you are doing. At ChristLife, we spend a half hour turning our hearts to the Lord in prayer for the work of ChristLife's ministry, and we end that time by asking for Mary's intercession. She knows exactly what it feels like to be too busy, to meet problems that have no obvious solution, to wonder whether your work will be successful. She also knows what it's like to surrender completely to God and to give yourself over to Christ in perfect obedience and trust. Ask her to make these gifts your own.

UNION WITH CHRIST

The Decree on the Apostolate of the Laity tells us something we should never forget: "The success of the lay apostolate depends on the laity's living union with Christ" (4). Write it down. Your work to advance the mission of the Church doesn't depend on your talents or fortuitous circumstances or generous levels of funding or finding the right colleagues. It depends on your union with Jesus.

Your union with Jesus isn't something mysterious and difficult to achieve. The Decree says it's "nourished by spiritual aids which are common to all the faithful, especially active participation in the sacred liturgy" (4). It's Basic Christian Living 101—all the topics covered in this book: prayer, Scripture, the sacraments, forgiveness, gifts of the Holy Spirit, and combatting the world, the flesh, and the devil. Make use of these practices and habits. They will draw you closer to Christ, and nourish the work given to you by God.

The Decree makes another important point: "Neither family concerns nor other secular affairs should be irrelevant to their spiritual life" (4). We might rewrite that sentence to say it positively: Family concerns and other secular affairs *are relevant* to our spiritual lives. There's no real separation between them. Family concerns and secular affairs are where we meet Christ. Secular affairs bring us into contact with people who need to hear the Gospel. We work within social institutions and use tools of communication to share the love of Christ. Some of us may be called to a mission field far away. But for the vast majority of us, our mission field is right where we are at this moment. Your mission is in your family, in the job you have, the parish you belong to, and the school you attend. It's on the sidelines of the soccer field, on the plane in which you're flying, and in the restaurant where you're eating lunch with a friend.

Serving Christ isn't easy. Jesus said, "If any man would come after me, let him deny himself and take up his cross daily and follow me" (Lk 9:23). Self-denial and suffering are part of the life of a disciple. We can meet difficulties with confidence and good cheer because the Lord is doing the work in us. As the Decree on the Apostolate of the Laity puts it: we forge ahead in "a happy and ready spirit, trying prudently and patiently to overcome difficulties" (4). Two qualities will serve us especially well. One is patience: "Let us run with perseverance the race that is set before us" (Heb 12:1). The other is gratitude: "And whatever you do, in word or deed, do everything in the name of the Lord Jesus, giving thanks to God the Father through him" (Col 3:17).

It's when we lose our life for the sake of Christ and His Kingdom that we find life and can carry the Kingdom of God and His presence into every situation. We only have one life to live. Let's give it for the sake of our Savior who gave it all for us. Empowered by the Spirit, with hearts full of gratitude, let's set forth to do what twelve apostles and a handful of other Christians did in the ancient world. Let's change the world. Let's do the work of Christ. Let's bring His love to everyone we meet.

PRACTICAL APPLICATION TO BECOME "DOERS OF THE WORD"

We have reviewed many areas of following Christ as His disciple. Take time to review how you are implementing the practices taught in this book. How are you doing? Let us know how you are growing as you follow Christ! We will be praying for you!

About ChristLife

ChristLife equips Catholics for the essential work of evangelization so others might personally encounter Jesus Christ and be transformed into His missionary disciples in the Catholic Church. The ministry partners with parishes, priests, religious, and lay leaders who are seeking to answer the Church's call for the New Evangelization through a proven method of parish evangelization and outreach. They developed the ChristLife Series to help all people discover, follow, and share Jesus Christ as members of the Catholic Church.

ChristLife's story began with Dave Nodar, a Catholic layman who during the 1990s regularly presented schools of evangelization in Poland and Slovakia for young adult Catholics from the former Soviet Bloc. Inspired by the call of Pope John Paul II to a new evangelization, Dave approached Cardinal William Keeler, Archbishop of Baltimore, about beginning an evangelization ministry. The Cardinal was enthused, and he recognized ChristLife as an apostolate of the Archdiocese in 1995.

Contact Us

600 Cooks Lane
Baltimore, MD 21229
(888) 498-8474
(443) 388-8910
info@christlife.org
www.christlife.org

Find Us on Social Media

Facebook ("ChristLifeOrg")

Twitter ("ChristLifeInc")

YouTube ("ChristLifeMinistry")

THE CHRISTLIFE SERIES

Discovering Christ

Discovering Christ is a seven-week experience that creates an open door in the parish for people who are searching for the meaning of their lives where they can share the Good News and the personal love of Jesus Christ. To learn more, visit: **www.christlife.org/discover**.

Following Christ

Following Christ is a seven-week journey that builds upon Discovering Christ and provides the tools to help Catholics grow in discipleship, including daily personal prayer, hearing God in Scripture, the power of the sacraments, forgiving one another, spiritual warfare, etc. To learn more, visit: **www.christlife.org/follow**.

Sharing Christ

Sharing Christ is a seven-week mission that equips Catholics with the practical skills to proclaim the Gospel, draw others into a personal relationship with Jesus Christ, and invite them to become His disciples as members of the Church. To learn more, visit: **www.christlife.org/share**.

ABOUT THE AUTHORS

Dave Nodar is the founder and director of ChristLife. For over forty years he has been a lay leader in renewal and evangelization in the Catholic Church.

Rev. Erik Arnold is a pastor in the Archdiocese of Baltimore, a member of the ChristLife board of directors, and ChristLife's liaison to the Archbishop of Baltimore.

Ally Ascosi is a wife and mother of four children who regularly volunteers with ChristLife and her parish. She graduated from Marymount University with a theology degree in 2007.